WHAT DO YOU WANT OUT OF LIFE?

WHAT DO YOU WANT OUT OF LIFE?

A PHILOSOPHICAL GUIDE TO FIGURING OUT WHAT MATTERS

VALERIE TIBERIUS

PRINCETON UNIVERSITY PRESS

PRINCETON AND OXFORD

Published by Princeton University Press
41 William Street, Princeton, New Jersey 08540
99 Banbury Road, Oxford OX2 6JX

press.princeton.edu

All Rights Reserved

First paperback printing, with discussion questions, 2024

Cloth ISBN 978-0-691-24068-8
Paperback ISBN 978-0-691-24139-5
E-book ISBN 978-0-691-24069-5

British Library Cataloging-in-Publication Data is available

Editorial: Rob Tempio and Chloe Coy
Production Editorial: Sara Lerner
Text Design: Heather Hansen
Jacket/Cover Design: Faceout Studio, Molly von Borstel
Production: Erin Suydam
Publicity: Maria Whelan and Carmen Jimenez
Copyeditor: Katherine Harper

This book has been composed in Baskerville with Novecento

Printed in the United States of America

For my sisters, Paula and Kiry

CONTENTS

Contents

PREFACE

I could not have been more surprised to discover that life doesn't sort itself out as you get older. That's what I thought in my twenties: that by the time I was in my fifties, I would have it all figured out. Sure, some things get more settled, your options shrink, you become more certain in some areas. But there are so many changes to adapt to that you never end up just coasting. This book is motivated by a desire to understand how we should think through our choices, goals, and values in the face of continual change. If there's no coasting, how do we keep moving so that our lives go as well as they can?

Of course, as I write this in 2022, continual change is also on my mind because of recent events. The COVID-19 pandemic and the near-collapse of American democracy gave us all a lot of new things to deal with. For those of us lucky enough to keep our jobs and to be relatively secure, the pandemic created a lot of doubt and worry. It has been easy to wonder about the point of doing whatever it is we're doing with so much of our time (teaching philosophy, in my case) when we're on the brink of disaster. These thoughts led me to think it would be worthwhile to write something that might be of interest to more than my typical audience of twenty academic philosophers. They also led me to think about how we anchor ourselves in times of upheaval—about the values that give us purpose and how we should think about them.

The truth is that I've always thought about these questions. What's new is just that I'm thirty years older than when I started. Being a philosopher, I thought there should be some philosophy to help me think about these topics. There is, but not as much as I thought. Ancient philosophy has some good stuff, but there have been some important changes in the last two thousand years. Recent philosophy has become so technical and specialized that I haven't found it that helpful. Also, so much of the kind of philosophy I have been trained to read was written by white men; when it comes to questions about how to live my life, I have often felt there are things we don't have in common. When I've heard white men talk about a midlife crisis, for example, it tends to be about coping with not being the Great Men they were told they would be. No one ever thought I would be a Great Man, so this hasn't been an issue for me. Many of the issues I *have* had are tied up in some way with sexism and bias. So this book is also motivated by a desire to write something about living a good life that is from a woman's point of view.

In the past decade or so, psychologists have more or less taken over from philosophers in writing about happiness. But I haven't found that psychological research answers my questions either. Much of the research is wonderful and interesting, but it doesn't give me a general way to think about how to live my life. Psychology has helped me figure out how to meet certain goals that I already have: I know that if I want to feel happier, for example, I should count my blessings, and that if I want to feel connected to other people, I should practice active constructive responding.[1] But psychology doesn't provide a general approach to thinking about life, nor has it helped me put all the different pieces of advice together.

What I have always liked about philosophy is its focus on the big questions and its unremitting effort to synthesize what we know about ourselves and the world. At its best, it can provide a coherent way of looking at things so that we can muddle through life more sensibly than we might otherwise. So this is a philosophical guide rather than a self-help book. It doesn't contain a ten-step program to happiness, wealth, or weight loss. Instead, it offers a way of thinking about what matters in life that helps us deal with the challenges of conflicting goals, lack of information, and an often uncooperative world.

As I write these words, I'm very conscious of the fact that the main obstacles to living well for most of the world's population come from external sources, not from inner conflict. Injustice, poverty, oppression, inadequate healthcare, unfair labor practices, and so on are enormous obstacles to living well. They raise complex political and economic questions that are not my expertise. I do think that those of us fortunate enough not to be impeded by such daunting external obstacles ought to think about our role in solving problems like these, and while this book isn't going to save the world, it does offer tools for thoughtful people to get their priorities straight.

Since philosophical thinking tends to be very abstract, I have tried to use a lot of examples to illustrate the theoretical points I make. Often, I use myself as an example, and I have to admit that talking about personal examples in this way feels strange to me, since it's not what philosophers usually do. Instead, we tend to talk about generic characters A and B who do generic actions like φ-ing and ψ-ing at time *t1* or *t2*. Sometimes we get more realistic and make up characters who have names (like Anna and Bob!), but it's not usual in the tradition in which I was raised to talk about one's own life in any detail. I don't think that thinly described examples of hypothetical people are good enough for this subject matter. The kind of process that is involved in understanding our goals and values depends heavily on the details of a person's life. So to illustrate the process in this book, I had to talk about experiences I know well enough to be familiar with those details. Fortunately, I'm fairly sure my experiences are not unique and I am hopeful that they will resonate with my readers. I've also tried to add less-detailed examples based on friends and people I've read about wherever I can.

One thing I talk about in some depth is being a woman in a field that hasn't been particularly welcoming to women. The experience of being marginalized is really not something that is discussed in the literature on happiness and well-being. Philosophers who write about well-being and happiness have tended to talk about generic individuals rather than women or men, Black people or Asian people, and so on. This seems to me problematic—at least when we try to apply our philosophy to the real world—because how we cope with our social world is tremendously important to how well we can flourish. It's useful to talk about the context of prejudice and oppressive socialization because we're better able to cope with something once we recognize how it affects us.

It is also tricky to talk about this context, because there are so many different experiences and I can only speak knowledgably about my own. As I write this, one year after George Floyd was murdered by a police officer in my city, Minneapolis, I am particularly conscious of the ways in which Black Americans' experience is different from mine. I chose to focus mainly on my own experience so that I could stick with what

I know to be true. But after reading the memoirs and calls to arms from many brilliant Black writers (James Baldwin, Ta-Nehisi Coates, Nikole Hannah-Jones, Ibram X. Kendi, Isabel Wilkerson[2]), I do think that there are some broad commonalities in the experiences of people who are coping with a world that doesn't want to let them do what they want to do. This doesn't mean that we know what it's like to be in each other's shoes (our experiences are often too different for that), but it might mean that we can benefit from the same kinds of strategies for coping with other people's prejudiced expectations, resisting the pressure to conform to a way of being that doesn't suit us, and refusing to think of ourselves in the way that we are defined by others. I hope that my writing allows readers to see the general point of my specific examples and substitute their own details to see how it applies to other lives.

ROADMAP

Philosophy can be hard to read. I know this from teaching and from talking to strangers who, when I tell them I teach philosophy, get a kind of grimace on their faces and report that they took a philosophy class once, but it was too hard. Academic philosophy—the kind that gets published in professional journals—is difficult, just as any academic writing can be. It's full of jargon and written for a specialized audience. I have tried to write this book without jargon for nonspecialists, but there may still be things about it that readers find challenging. Philosophers tend to make a lot of distinctions, to define terms in very specific and sometimes unusual ways, and to expect readers to remember all this throughout their lengthy arguments. As much as I've tried to write for nonphilosophers, I know I haven't avoided these hallmarks of philosophical writing entirely. So I thought it would be useful to start with a summary of the main argument (including some definitions of key terms) that readers can come back to as needed.

In the briefest possible terms, this is a book about value fulfillment and strategies for achieving it in the face of conflict. My starting point is that we human beings are valuing creatures who do well when we achieve the things we care about in life. Conflicts among our values and goals pull us in competing directions, away from fulfillment. Conflicts between our goals and the world frustrate our pursuits and lead us (again) away from fulfillment. Our lives go better for us when we can figure out ways of managing these conflicts, and good management requires a good understanding of what we care about in the first place.

This brief description has already used some special terminology, so let's back up and start with some definitions. In the preface, I've talked about "what matters to us" and "what we care about." In the rest of the book, I use the terms "values" and "goals" to refer to these things. Basically, goals are the things we want. More technically, they are representations of a better state of affairs than the one we're in. The category of goals is very, very large: it includes widely shared things such as food, water, shelter, and sex, but also very specific things like "a piece of Margaret's ginger cheesecake" and "replacing the lightbulb in my closet." Our multifarious goals are organized into a rough and messy hierarchy. There are some things we want for the sake of other things. I want the cheesecake and the lightbulb for the sake of other goals, namely, the delicious taste and being able to see my clothes. Others we want for their own sake, like the health and happiness of my family. Even among our most basic goals, some are more important than others.

Values, as I define them, are special goals. They tend to be more "ultimate" (rather than "instrumental"), in the sense that we want to achieve them for their own sakes. They also tend to be important to us and, ideally, well integrated into our psychology. In other words, values are goals that are high up in our hierarchy and ones we are not internally conflicted about. For me, the goal of a piece of cheesecake is in conflict with the goal of managing my type 1 diabetes, whereas I am not very conflicted about the value of health. I want cheesecake, but I *value* my health.

I just said that values are "ideally" well integrated. This will raise some questions. Am I saying that some values are better for us than others? Yes, I am! And that leads me to our central topic.

This book is shaped by two main questions:

(a) How do we identify our values and goals and recognize the conflicts between them?
(b) How can our values and goals be improved so we can manage these conflicts and promote greater fulfillment?

Identifying values and resolving conflicts is a little like gardening. To be honest, I hate gardening, but I have enough gardeners in my circle of friends and family to have a sense of what goes on with them. Gardeners work with what they've got—the soil, grown trees, the shape of the plot of land—and make it into something satisfying. For some people, this will mean a garden that produces fruit; for others, it will mean a garden that looks nice; for others, it might mean a garden that can't be ruined by cavorting dogs. Plants come into conflict: trees with dense foliage create shade in which other plants can't grow, some trees (like the black walnut) are toxic to lots of other plants, and some plants are invasive and take over everything. The gardener has to navigate these conflicts: find the best spots for the prized plants, remove the weeds, and sometimes make peace with imperfection.

Going with this metaphor, life is a garden, our goals are plants, and our values are the plants we care most about. What we need to do is to figure out what we've got to work with, which are our most prized goals (our values), and how to put everything together in a way that works for us. In gardening, if your black walnut tree is killing everything in your garden, you can cut it down or you can change your expectations about what kinds of plants you can grow under it. If your expensive rose bush is dying from soggy soil, you can change the soil or choose a different varietal that's more tolerant of muck. Values can be approached in a similar way. If your commitment to running marathons is ruining your joints and taking time away from your family, you may need to find a new way of thinking about competition and fitness. Yank marathons and replace them with walking. If your approach to friendship requires that you sacrifice all of your own interests in order to do what your friend wants to do, maybe you need to rethink what being a good friend requires—or find friends who are less demanding than a finicky rose.

Figuring out what matters to us is the focus of chapter 3. There, we'll talk about several different strategies for learning about our values and goals: introspection, the lab rat strategy (studying yourself from the outside), guided reflection, learning from others, and exploration.

Chapters 4, 5, and 6 tackle managing conflicts among our goals, including those special goals called "values." We'll start in chapter 4 by distinguishing three different types of conflict: inner conflict about a single goal, conflict among different goals, and conflict between our goals and the environment. Then we'll talk about three basic responses to conflict:

1. Prioritize and adjust means to ends
2. Give up one of the conflicting goals
3. Reinterpret our values.

Conflict management gets complicated when we add an uncooperative world. These challenges of context are discussed in chapter 5. Then, in chapter 6, we add two more possible responses to conflict:

4. Make peace with what you can't change
5. Consider radical change.

So far, it may look as though the book is entirely about our first question (How do we identify our values and goals and recognize the conflicts between them?). But this impression is misleading, because the process of identifying our values cannot be neatly separated from the process of figuring out what it would be good for us to value. As we investigate our goals and values, we often find that we don't have a very clear picture of exactly what they are and what it means to succeed in terms of them. For example, we know we value "work," but we might find ourselves unsure whether we really care about developing and using our skills, making a meaningful contribution to a larger organization, or earning the respect of our peers. As we try to clarify what matters to us and encounter problematic conflicts, we have choices about how to understand and prioritize our goals and values. We can't make these choices without thinking about what would make our lives better or worse. Understanding and improvement are part of the same process.

What improvement looks like varies from person to person. I am not going to give you a list of values you must have. I wouldn't want to tell you which plants to buy, either. There is so much individual variation—in our goal hierarchies and our plant preferences—that this would not be a helpful approach. However, we can identify some general guidelines for thinking about the question of what values are good to have. First, almost all of us, as products of human evolution, have basic psychological motivations toward comfort and security, novelty and excitement, autonomy (control over our own lives), competence (the skills to do what we want to do), and affiliation with other people. Second, as we develop, these basic drives are shaped by our personalities and our environments (caretakers, teachers, culture, and so on) into specific goals. The guideposts of human nature and individual psychological nature influence how we can change our values. They don't prevent change altogether, but they do shape what kind of change is possible for us. And this means that, to see how our values could be improved, we have to take account of what we are like.

The *best* values for us, then, are the ones that suit who we are and that we can actually realize in our lives. One important fact about who we are is that human beings are a profoundly social species. For the most part, we flourish together in families, friendships, and communities. This means that the best values for us are going to involve other people in some significant ways. Because social relationships are so important, the values of friendship, family, and community come up throughout the book, but we'll focus on them explicitly in chapters 7 and 8. These chapters consider how we ought to treat others and where moral values fit into our gardens.

That's the roadmap. I hope you enjoy the journey!

WHAT DO YOU WANT OUT OF LIFE?

1

WHAT WE WANT AND WHAT STANDS IN OUR WAY

I am a so-called nice person. I was raised in Canada, so I'm culturally polite. My lifelong type 1 diabetes taught me that disappointing people (doctors, especially) will probably result in my death. When I was growing up in the 1970s, my feminist parents taught me that I could do whatever I wanted, but still, many of my cultural role models were fairly traditional: men were leaders and women were helpers. I'm a pleaser and I'm deeply conflict-averse. I'm also a philosopher. Philosophy attracts and rewards people who have the virtues of fighters— people who are combative and quick on their feet. I'm not a fighter. Especially when I was younger, I spent most of my time listening to debates and thinking about why both sides were right in a way. This often made me feel as though I wasn't cut out for philosophy, despite how much I loved reading and thinking about "big" questions. My nice personality was not the best fit for a field that prizes holding your ground against aggressive intellectuals who often seem more interested in winning the point than exploring the issue.

This lack of fit has been a problem for me. It has made it more difficult to do the things that matter to me, such as being a nice person and a good philosopher. There was even a time when I became quite an unpleasant person. When I was in graduate school—prime time for learning how to fit in—I would argue like a lawyer at otherwise peaceful family dinners. I can still hear my sister Paula's words ringing in my ears: "Not every conversation is about winning or being right about something!" Training to be a philosopher made me worse at being a good sister.

I'll admit that I have never felt entirely at home in philosophy. I have felt stupid and like a fraud. At various times, I have not felt taken seriously and I have felt that my questions and ideas were just a little "off." A friend once advised me to "gore the ox" in my philosophical writing as a way to get published more easily. He meant that I should identify an enemy position and kill it with a devastating objection before offering my own ideas on the topic. I tried, but I'm just not much good with a stick and I'm never very motivated to harm the ox. (I think of the arguments with my family as inept attempts to gore the wrong animal.) I can say from experience that time spent feeling like an imposter and worrying that you are in the wrong field is time not spent doing your job and getting better at it.

If I had been less concerned with pleasing other people, or if I had been more interested in a career in which pleasing people was a positive, I could have skipped along happily doing what I wanted. Instead, this conflict between my "nice personality" and my career was a wrench in the works that caused me to wonder about what I was doing. What's so great about philosophy, I thought, if so many philosophers are mean and don't actually listen to each other in their rush to prove their own point? What's so great about being nice if it causes me so much anxiety about whether I've said the wrong thing and hurt someone's feelings? I had, in effect, a crisis of values that made me unsure what to do. Should I quit and do something else? Should I take lorazepam? Uncertainty about what matters to you makes it hard to move forward. If you don't really know what you want, it's hard to know how to get it.

This conflict from my life is fairly ordinary. It has never been life or death; it's not an existential crisis that drove me to drugs or caused major depression. Also, while the details are particular to me, the broad outline—a conflict between incompatible goals that drives people to wonder what they're doing with their lives—is not uncommon at all. Many of these conflicts involve our jobs: You want to be a good parent and to be successful in your career, but both things compete for your time. You want to make a lot of money, but moving up the ladder in your company means spending time with people you don't like. You want your work to be ethical, but you're really good at defending corporations from environmental protection lawsuits. You're offered your dream job, but it's a thousand miles away from your family. You're torn between a job that pays well enough and leaves you time to go to the gym, or a job you find more fulfilling but that will take a toll on your fitness. Work/life balance, as it has been called, is a prime example of one of these ordinary conflicts, but it's not the only one.

Because we have many goals, we also face many possibilities for conflict. Say, for example, that you are committed to your church, but you have a gay friend and the church takes a position on gay marriage that you cannot accept. Or that you and your partner are having trouble conceiving a child, and you are conflicted between in vitro fertilization and adoption. Or that you want to give your child every opportunity, but driving them to lessons and clubs every day of the week leaves you with no time for yourself.[1] Or that you want to learn to tap dance, but you were brought up to think that dancing is a frivolous waste of time. There are as many possibilities as there are people.

All of these conflicts can cause us to wonder whether we're on the right track. Is the work you do at your company worth the sacrifice? Does being a good parent really demand so much driving? How important is money? What is it you value about your church, and could you get it from a different church? Serious conflicts raise questions about the things we value. But even before that happens, conflicts show up in life as stress, frustration, and unhappiness. Chances are that, if things aren't going well, you can find some conflict at the bottom of it.

Now, it's worth clarifying that not everything we would call a conflict is a problem. I'm conflicted about the choice between ginger cheesecake and pumpkin cheesecake, and this doesn't cause me much grief. Minor conflict or friction between our goals can even be beneficial: pursuing very different goals may enrich our understanding of each of them, and confronting conflict can promote creative thinking about new ways to put things together. The kinds of conflicts that we're focusing on in this book are the ones that inhibit our success in terms of what really matters to us. We could call these "serious conflicts," but I won't always add the qualifier. The examples in the following chapters should clarify what kinds of conflicts are the problem.

This book is about serious conflicts, then, and how to manage them in ways that make our lives better and satisfy our reflective minds. It does not prescribe a particular program or set of rules to follow. I believe that different solutions work for different people and that the best a philosopher can do is to identify the problem, articulate a general solution, and point to a number of ways we might reach that solution. The general solution requires thinking about what really matters to us, given our nature, and refining our goals so that they are *not* in serious conflict. It's therefore also a book about how to figure out what matters. Exactly how to do this in practice—with help from a friend or a therapist, by journaling and making lists, through meditation—depends on what you're like as an individual, your particular skills and weaknesses. What you'll find in the pages that follow is a general philosophical approach to thinking about our values, our goals, and how they fit together in a life.

GOAL CONFLICT AND THE HUMAN CONDITION

Compare the situation of creatures like us to the situation of my little dog, Sugar. Sugar's life also goes well for her when she can get the things that matter to her, namely belly rubs, control of the dog beds, and snacks. There isn't much else she wants.

The human condition, on the other hand (at least for any human being who is reading this book), is vastly more complicated. As babies, we may start out with goals that are similar to Sugar's, but our sophisticated brains and built-in curiosity quickly move us beyond these basic needs. We develop into people with diverse, multifaceted, interrelated goals. We don't stop wanting affection and food, but these basic goals become much less basic as we learn about the norms and expectations of our cultures and families. The need for food turns into a love of haute cuisine, authentic barbeque, or vegan cooking. Our need for affection is entangled with the ideals of relationships shaped by our culture. We become people with demanding checklists for mates, rebellious ideas about what types of friends we may have, fantasies of traditional weddings that don't align with our feminist values, or strong commitments to caring about a chosen (rather than biological) family. And, of course, the development of our complex system of goals isn't confined to food and affection. As we discover what we enjoy, what we're good at, and what we're able to do, we add more and more goals and subgoals: work, financial security, sports, music, art, writing, reading, playing games, worship, volunteer work, teaching, learning a language, and so on.

We are also consciously aware of the fact that we have goals, which means that we are capable of examining, doubting, favoring, or rejecting at least some of them. Sugar does experience conflicts, but she (almost certainly) doesn't have conflicts between what she wants and what she thinks about what she wants. She never *doubts* whether belly rubs are worth the trouble or *wonders* if eating poop will be bad for her in the long run. There is no wrench in the works for a beagle, nothing that gives her pause and forces reconsideration of what matters in life.

Of course, we are not always aware of our goals, and we are never aware of all of them at the same time. If someone asked you what your goals are, you could probably think of something to say. You might say that you are working on reducing your blood pressure, or that you're trying to learn to swim, or that you're looking for a job you like that pays decently. But we do not go around in life with a detailed list of goals foremost in our minds. One reason for this is that our brains are so complex that much of what happens there does so without our conscious attention. This means that, in addition to whatever goals we are aware of, we also have hidden goals—goals we are not attending to consciously—that move us to do things and cause all sorts of feelings, from frustration to contentment. My desire to please has often been a hidden goal. It has affected what I do and how I feel about interacting with people, even when I've been entirely unaware of it. People with strong motivations to please others likely have hidden goals to choose friends, careers, and lifestyles that are approved by their cultures.

Strong biological needs also function as hidden goals. An astronaut who chooses to spend a year in space without any human contact may experience great sadness due to hidden goals of affiliation that she has consciously decided to put on hold. This example lets us see that a single goal can be present to our conscious minds at one time but hidden from us at another. The astronaut may have been very much aware of the goal of forming close relationships with other people while she was dating in college. But when she decides to concentrate on space exploration for a while, she turns her focus away from relationships, not seeing it as an important goal at the moment. And yet the goal of relationships may still be there, hidden but powerful enough to cause an emotional reaction to isolation. We could think of conscious attention as a flashlight with limited reach: it illuminates some of our goals and brings them to conscious awareness, but many of them remain in the dark until we change our focus.

We'll talk more about this process of illuminating our goals in the following chapters. For now, we can just acknowledge that it's no wonder that the human condition is characterized by conflict. There are just too many moving pieces for all of them to fit together in a harmonious way. Does this matter? I think it matters tremendously.

Like my beagle, human beings are animals, and our lives also go well when we can achieve our goals and do the things that matter to us. Serious conflict stands in the way. This is for two reasons. First, conflict between goals makes it more difficult for us to succeed and get what we want. When we have a conflict, working toward one goal takes away from—or even goes against—working toward another. This is a problem we share with other creatures: Sugar can't both hunt for poopsicles and get a belly rub at the same time. But for most other animals, conflicts are easily resolved as one desire naturally overtakes another. This is sometimes true for humans: eventually my desire for delicious cheesecake will force a decision between ginger and pumpkin. But we also have conflicts that are not easily resolved, and these get in our way. Second, for humans, serious conflict can prompt reflection on whether we have the right goals at all. When we feel internally conflicted, constantly frustrated, or pulled in different directions, we may wonder if we're just barking up the wrong tree. Let me explain both of these points more carefully, since they are an important motivation for the rest of the book.

It's easiest to see how conflict frustrates the very goals that fuel it. To put it as simply as possible, if you want to eat an apple and you want to avoiding eating apples, one of these goals will have to be frustrated. Similarly, if my being a successful philosopher demands that I give up being a nice person, then I can't meet both of my goals at once. If either learning to speak Spanish or learning to carve wooden ducks would take up all of your free time, then you can't do both. If being a good parent means staying at home with your child, then you cannot both be a good parent and have a demanding career. Now, learning to carve ducks may not take up all your free time, and being a good parent may not mean staying at home. As we'll see, there is room for reinterpreting our goals so that they are *not* in conflict (that's part of the general solution to our problem). But my point is that if the way you conceive of your goals puts them in conflict, then you will be less successful at meeting them.

Conflict also frustrates the pursuit of *other* goals that don't even seem to be connected. When conflict produces bad feelings like anxiety and stress, which it very often does, it frustrates goals that almost all of us have: health and happiness. Conflict is uncomfortable and demands our attention, which takes time away from other things that are more important.

Conflicts often stand in the way of our altruistic goals, too. Think about the advice to "put on your own mask before assisting others." This started as an instruction for airplane passengers, but it has now become a self-care meme. Not having your own house in order makes it difficult to help others; people who are stressed and miserable and torn up with inner conflicts are typically not the most supportive spouses, parents, or friends. A person who is able to do what she values, without debilitating conflict, has more of the resources needed to be helpful. She has more oxygen.

So, the first problem with conflict (when it's persistent and unresolved) is that it makes it harder to achieve many of our goals. The second problem is that conflict can unsettle our busy, reflective minds and make us uncertain about what we really want. If you're pulled in two conflicting directions, you have to decide which way to go. If we're lucky, the solution is obvious to us, but often we're not sure. This is a problem because, in order to pursue your goals, you need to know what they are and which ones should be prioritized. Conflict makes us wonder if we really do know this. I described how this happened in my own case: I found myself wondering whether philosophy was really the right career for me or whether my personality was a product of sexist culture that I should try to overcome. Similarly, conflicts between a taxing job and a demanding family can cause people to wonder about the point of career success, or about the soundness of their standards for being a good spouse or parent.

We might pause here and ask: What's so important about fulfilling our goals? To some people, this will seem like a silly question: what could be worse than not being able to do what you want to do? But to others, this is a deep philosophical question about the nature of a good human life, one that philosophers have been trying to answer for thousands of years.[2] Throughout history, some philosophers have said that a good life—also referred to as *well-being* or flourishing—is a life with many pleasures and few pains; the good life is all about our feelings, according to these hedonists, and it's better to feel good than bad. Others have argued that a good life is one in which we live up to our human potential by developing our capacities for reason and moral virtue. Recently, psychologists have entered the fray with their own ideas about what makes life good. Some agree with the hedonist philosophers that feeling good and feeling satisfied with life is what it's all about. Others talk about the importance of satisfying basic human needs for self-direction, relationships, and developing skills.[3]

My own view about well-being is that it is best understood as the fulfillment of the values that fit our personalities and our circumstances.[4] We do well when we succeed in terms of what matters to us, and when what matters to us suits our desires, emotions, and judgments. If that's what well-being is, it's easy to see why fulfilling goals is important—my theory of well-being just defines it in terms of the fulfillment of a special set of important goals called "values." There's nothing more to living well than fulfilling your important and psychologically fitting goals. This is the value fulfillment theory of well-being.

One concern you might have about this theory is that, if a good life is just fulfilling your values, then a terrible person might do perfectly well pursuing values that are great for them, but awful for us. This is a thorny issue, for sure, and some philosophers take this to be a deal-breaker for theories like mine. I have two things to say in response. As we will see later, the value fulfillment theory does not make it easy for someone with immoral values to achieve well-being. For most people, morally good values contribute to well-being. In addition, my view has some advantages precisely because it does *not* have an objective standard for which values are the right ones. For one thing, it avoids the very difficult task of proving what such an objective standard might be. For another, it avoids the one-size-fits-all approach to thinking about good human lives. Given how different people can be from each other, I think this is quite important.

That said, you don't have to agree with me about the nature of well-being to agree with me about the importance of fulfilling our goals. We can put these philosophical debates aside. This is because no matter what you think a good life is, no matter how you answer the ancient question about the nature of human flourishing, you will have to make it your goal to achieve it. The way that we pursue a good life—no matter how it is defined—is by having goals, figuring out plans for attaining them, and acting on those plans. If you think that human well-being consists in achieving certain objective goods such as knowledge, friendship, or a relationship with God, then you have to figure out what it means to acquire knowledge, be a good friend, or develop a relationship with God, and you have to aim at these things in your actions. Things that conflict with these goals and prevent you from achieving them are bad for you. If you agree with the hedonists that the good life is just the pleasant life, then your goal is to seek pleasure and shun pain; conflict with this goal will frustrate your attempt to live well. No matter how you think about human flourishing or well-being, you can't avoid the importance of goals and goal conflict.

THE BASIC APPROACH

We do better in life when we acknowledge our most important ultimate goals and find ways to pursue all of our goals so that they fit better together. I call these most important ultimate goals "values." The way that I understand "values" is that they are the aims that are very important to us, the ones we think about when we reflect on how our life is going. If someone were to ask you right now to reflect on the state of your life, what would you think about? Personally, I would think about how I've been feeling, my mood, my family, my marriage, my friendships, my health, my job, my contribution to the state of the world—and then my assessment of how things are going for me in general would be based on how things are going in these areas of my life.[5] These things (happiness, relationships, teaching, health) are my values. Life goes well for us when we fulfill our *values*, then, and this requires strategies for dealing with inevitable serious conflicts. These strategies enable us to do what matters to us and also to arrive at an understanding of what matters that gives us confidence that we're on the right path.

This basic approach shares certain assumptions with Existentialism, a philosophy that emphasizes individual choice and freedom. Existentialism holds that there are no absolute values imposed from outside of us, but instead that things matter because they matter *to us*. This book also works from that assumption: that there is value in the world because there are people who value things, and that what we need to do in life is figure out what to value and how. I also share the Existentialist assumption that we have some latitude in choosing our goals and actions. We have more than Sugar the beagle, who is driven entirely by her desires for snacks and comfort. The fact that we have some choice about how we understand, prioritize, and pursue our goals means that there is room to make better choices. This will be an important point throughout the book: as we think about our current goals and try to resolve conflicts among them, we are at the same time looking for ways to improve the system of goals that we have.

I part company with the Existentialists on their idea of "radical" choice. Existentialism holds that there is no essential human nature that constrains our choices and so we must think of ourselves as fundamentally free to choose the values that define who we are. Instead, I think that our choices about values are made in the context of our goal-seeking psychology and our highly social, interdependent human nature.[6] We are not radical choosers, because our choices are bound by what we are like. To go back to the metaphor I introduced in the "Roadmap" section, we make choices about what plants to grow in our gardens within the limits of our zone, average rainfall, soil quality, and so on. By the time we're able to reflect on our own values and consider changes, we have been shaped quite profoundly by our upbringing and culture. It wouldn't make sense to just root out everything we care about and start from scratch! Even before culture and upbringing get to work on us, most human beings have strong innate tendencies to value such things as relationships, feeling happy, and acting autonomously in ways that use our skills. We may not be "driven" by these basic needs in the way that Sugar is driven by hers, but they provide guideposts for our choices. And, as we'll see, it's not a bad thing to have guideposts.

2

WHAT TURTLES, DOGS, AND PEOPLE HAVE IN COMMON

I'm sure many women have had the experience of looking for a pair of shoes to match the dress they bought to wear to some event, like a wedding. For me, anyway, this experience is actually full of conflicting goals. I want shoes that look great with the dress, don't hurt my feet, don't cost a fortune, and can be worn again. That's really four different goals! When we shop, we have to balance these goals, sacrificing perfection here for a little bit more satisfaction there. If we're completely unwilling to sacrifice anything, we may end up going to the wedding barefoot (or in frumpy old shoes that don't match the dress). If we sacrifice too much, we'll regret that we didn't spend just a little bit more time searching. But typically, this kind of conflict doesn't create a huge challenge for us. The main goal (shoes!) and the subgoals (appearance, comfort, affordability) are reasonably clear and they don't invite uncertainty and self-scrutiny. This could change if you really can't afford a new pair of shoes, or if you have so many pairs that you are on the verge of a shoe "problem."

Shopping entails relatively easy conflicts. There are others: What should I have for lunch? I want something healthy, tasty, and fast, and these definitely conflict, given what's in my fridge. Should I get paper or plastic? Paper might be more environmentally friendly, but plastic can be used for dog poop. The kinds of conflicts I'm talking about in this book are not easy—they are "serious"—but they are similar in two ways. We can identify subgoals or features of the goals involved in our major conflicts, too, and balancing these is crucial to success. In our ordinary, easy conflicts, we do this balancing without a whole lot of thought. The tough conflicts do require thought, and that's what we'll explore in the rest of the book. We won't abandon the simple conflicts completely, though. It will sometimes be helpful to see how things work in a simple case before we examine a more complex one.

What makes the tough conflicts more challenging than the easy conflicts? Why isn't life like shopping? The main thing is that some goals are just more important to us than others: we care more about them and we put them higher in our hierarchy of goals. This is easy to see. For most of us, making sure your children are fed and clothed is more important than learning to skateboard, and it's way more important than finding the right shoes for a wedding. Being financially secure is more important than enjoying cheesecake. Avoiding a deadly plague is more important than going to a bar for drinks. We have many different kinds of goals and they are not all at the same level of importance. There's nothing wrong with shoes, skateboarding, cheesecake, or going to a bar, but these goals are outweighed by their competitors. When important goals conflict with each other, and it's not easy to see a resolution, we have trouble.

Another factor that makes some conflicts more difficult than the shopping case has to do with the consequences of one goal for others. Some goals have greater impact on the rest of our goals. If I decide not to buy any shoes for the wedding and show up wearing frumpy pumps, my life will not be greatly affected. My friends would still love me. I would not lose my job. My health would not suffer. On the other hand, if I were to abandon my career goals because they conflict with my wanting to spend more time with my family, there would be many significant consequences. I would not have an income, I would lose my identity as a professor, and many of my professional relationships would suffer. Not much in my life is changed when I choose a plastic bag over a paper one, but there would be serious repercussions if I were to stop caring about my health. Not only would I likely live a shorter life (which would frustrate many of my long-term goals), but my friendships that are partly based on mutual athleticism would deteriorate. The more consequences our goals have for other goals, the more difficult the conflict.

These two features—importance and impact—are present in different degrees in various of our goals, especially those concerning our careers and relationships. They make conflicts much more difficult to solve than the ones we encounter when we shop for shoes. Dealing with them begins with identifying our most important goals, which I call "values."

Very briefly, for now, I define values as ultimate, important goals that are relatively well integrated into our psychology. In other words, they are goals that are high up in our hierarchy of goals and "fit" who we are. I *value* my relationship with my parents; calling each of them on the phone once a week is a goal. The best values for us to have are ones that can be fulfilled or realized together over time, because fulfilling our values is necessary for living a good life. Conflict among goals prevents us from fulfilling our values and therefore from living good lives. I want to show how identifying our values helps us to manage our conflicts so that they don't hurt us. But first it will be useful to have some more details about the nature of goals and values.

THE PSYCHOLOGY OF GOALS

What are goals? Goals are basically just mental representations of where we want to be. It is characteristic of animals, including human beings, that we want things, we think about how to get them, we try, we evaluate our success or failure, and we do this over and over again. Psychologists call creatures like this "goal-directed, self-regulating systems" or—for the sci-fi fans among you—"cybernetic systems."[1] To get the idea, think of Millicent the turtle, a relatively simple self-regulating creature, even simpler than my beagle. Millicent lives in a stream and wants to eat the strawberries growing on the other side of the road. The strawberry is the goal, or the "reference value." It's called a reference value because it is used as the reference for determining what to do and whether the chosen course of action was successful. The reference value is a representation of an improvement on the current situation: it's better to be eating a strawberry! A self-regulating system must also have capacities to perceive how things are now and to compare the reference value to the current state of affairs. Millicent sees that she currently has no strawberries to eat (this is the "input" to the system), and she sees that this is less desirable than "strawberry," her reference value. Millicent then decides to cross over to the strawberry patch (this behavior is the "output"), where she happily eats to her turtley heart's content. The delightful taste of the berries and the nice feeling of a full belly become the new input to the system. Good feelings are important to the goal-seeking process: they reinforce learning. Pleasure is the reward for having found a way to achieve our goals. Millicent learns that she can cross the road, and that strawberries are good, and a new goal (getting back to the stream) arises.

Before you close this book in disgust, let me reassure you that I know we are not turtles. (Let me also confess that I don't know much about turtles, but nothing depends on the details of turtle behavior here.) Human self-regulating systems are far more complicated. The stages of the self-regulating system don't necessarily occur in this neat linear order: we can have multiple goals that we pursue at the same time, and so on. But this simple picture does provide us with a way to understand goals that I have found very helpful: goals are representations of a better state of affairs than the one we're in, a state that is preferred to the status quo. They guide our actions and what we learn from experience about how to go on.

This simple picture helps us in two ways. First, it helps explain what's wrong with conflict. Conflicting goals are a wrench in the works of a self-regulating goal-seeking system. How can you choose a course of action, evaluate its success, and learn from your experience if you are pulled in two directions at the same time? What happens to Millicent if she has the goal of crossing the road to eat the strawberries *and* the goal of staying near the stream? She can't do both at once. Fortunately, if Millicent is a well-functioning turtle, her conflict will be easily resolved. As her hunger increases and decreases, these two goals will switch places in order of importance. But if this didn't happen—if she wanted to stay and go to exactly the same degree all the time—she would be like Buridan's Ass, the mythical donkey who starved to death because he couldn't decide whether to eat the hay on the left or the right. Buridan's Turtle would likely be hit by a car, frozen between going for the strawberries and returning to the stream.

The second benefit of this psychological understanding of goals is that it allows us to understand the importance of hidden (nonconscious) goals, which will also be very important in what's to come. Goals need not be accessible to our conscious processing—your brain can represent something as a good state of affairs without your explicitly acknowledging that you have a goal. These hidden psychological goals and feelings are vague and difficult to express in language, but they are important influences on the self-regulating systems that control our actions. This is to be expected, given what we know about how the brain works. Conscious goals—like any conscious experience—use our working memory, and working memory is very limited compared to the overall capacity of our brains. If all of our goals were conscious, our working memory would be completely overwhelmed.[2]

One source of these nonconscious goals is our evolved goal-seeking nature. A goal-seeker—whether it's a turtle, a beagle, or a human being—has to have certain motivations to keep it going. If we are going to have goals, make an effort to attain them, and learn from our experience, we need to have some drive to explore the world and move beyond the status quo. But curiosity and exploration unchecked by stability will get us killed. We also need a built-in motivation toward stability and security. Stability without exploration, however, would have us starving in our caves. We need both goals: a push toward the world and a pull back home. We human beings are especially *social* goal-seeking creatures who need to work together to survive, so we also have evolved motivations to bond with each other.[3] These evolved goals—for novelty and excitement, comfort and security, and affiliation with other people—I will call our *basic psychological motivations*. They will be important in what's to come, because they are the steady backdrop against which we can arrange our goals and values to make our lives better.

No one is surprised about the existence of nonconscious forces when it comes to our biological goals like breathing, swallowing, and digesting. These are not conscious processes—and thank goodness for that: imagine if you had to put breathing and digesting on your already crowded to-do list! But people are more resistant to the idea of hidden forces when it comes to the goals that we pursue through our own actions. We are inclined to be impressed by our powers of conscious rational deliberation, choice, and planning. Philosophers have been particularly prone to this: Plato had the idea that our power of reason was like a charioteer sitting on top and in control of our impulses and feelings. But many of us (not just philosophers) like to think of ourselves as in charge of our own lives, not pushed around by forces beneath the surface.

It is a testament to our powers of self-deception that we are able to maintain this flattering self-image, given how much experience we have with the influence of hidden psychological forces on our actions. At least when we're talking about *other* people, hidden feelings that influence their conscious goals are quite familiar. We see that hidden feelings of self-doubt cause people to choose less ambitious goals or to give up on their dreams, shame causes people to avoid social interactions, and hidden desire for approval causes people to choose paths that please only their parents. The COVID-19 pandemic taught us something about the importance of our need for connectedness with other humans. The first time I hugged a friend after having hugged only my husband and my dogs for about six months, I burst into tears. And many people I know were surprised to find that when the pandemic eased up and we could socialize, we were deliriously happy to be together. Of course, we knew we were missing things in the preceding months, but I think our bodies knew better than we did how much those social goals were being frustrated while we were in lockdown.

We can sometimes see the influence of hidden goals in our own lives, though it typically takes some time to work out what was hidden. Many years ago, a close friend pointed out to me that in social conversations, I was more attentive to men than to women. As a good feminist, I felt immediately defensive, but this was a trusted friend who has some social skills, and she put it in a nice enough way that I could let it sink in. Over the years, I have come to see that, although I would never acknowledge paying more attention to what men say as one of my goals, I behaved in ways that revealed this hidden goal. Once I saw that, I could begin to train myself out of it. I suspect this is not terribly uncommon (for men or women). Research shows that men talk more than women do, though women are *perceived* to talk more.[4] One explanation for this is that many of us are drawn to what men have to say by subconscious bias and to regard what women have to say as interference with the important stuff.

In short, we have nonconscious psychological goals and other hidden forces that influence what we choose to do and how we do it. It's easy for us to believe this about other people, because we see so many examples of it. Given that each of us is a human being with a human brain, we should accept it about ourselves, too.

Before we move on to values, I want to address a concern that may be occurring to some readers. You might be worried that this simple picture of human beings as goal-seeking creatures is very "type A." Type A people are goal-focused, high-achieving workaholics obsessed with time management. The focus on goals may seem like a focus on achievement or "getting things done." Full disclosure: I have sometimes been accused of being type A. Maybe I've just written a book for people like me! I don't think so, though. The focus on our goal-seeking nature is only limited this way if our goals are similarly limited. Goals are how we represent the way we would like things to be, so they can include all sorts of things that are not type A. Your goal might be to spend more time living "in the moment," to put your work aside and relax with your friends, or, indeed, to become less type A.

VALUES: A SPECIAL TYPE OF GOAL

So, goals are desirable states of affairs that serve as a target for our actions and a standard for whether those actions succeeded. When two goals conflict, it means that achieving one of them comes at the cost of achieving another. What can we do about conflict? In broad outline, once we have identified our goals and seen the conflict, what we need to do is prioritize and compromise. We can see this in our shoe shopping case: unless I'm very lucky, I'll need to figure out how much comfort I'm willing to sacrifice for how much cuteness and cost, and vice versa. Or, think about lunch. I want to eat something that's healthy, tasty, and available. For me, sadly, taste and health often pull in different directions. Being a diabetic with a penchant for cheesecake and chocolate is not an easy life! I often decide to prioritize health and then choose the tastiest available thing within the domain of things that aren't terrible for me. But sometimes I put taste first and deprioritize health significantly. Either way, I'm making compromises, and different compromises depending on the occasion.

Even in the simple shopping and eating cases, it can be tricky to prioritize and compromise, as anyone who has gone down the rabbit hole of online shopping will know. In the more complex cases, in which the goals are more important and consequential, things are much more difficult. When we're dealing with conflicts between career and family, religion and politics, work and leisure, or the like, we may not even have a clear sense of what our goals and subgoals are. Prioritizing and compromising will also be much more challenging when it comes to these broad and important goals. In shopping or eating, we have a place to start: we want shoes, or we want to eat. With major life conflicts, we aren't even always sure what we want.

We need a place to start, and I propose that the place to start is with our *values*. Values are our most important goals, and they help with goal conflicts because they tell us what we should prioritize and what we need to attend to in our efforts to compromise.

What are values? To understand, we can start by thinking about what it is to value something. If you're like me, you probably value your friendships. What does this involve? In short, it involves desires, emotions, and thoughts. Valuing friendship means that I want to spend time with my friends; I feel happy when they're around and sad when I can't see them. I think that friendship is important to my life going well, and I think I should plan my life in a way that makes room for friendship. All three of these elements—desires, emotions, and thoughts—are important to valuing in the fullest sense. What do we think about a friend who claims that friendship is really important to her, but never calls or has any time for us when we want to hang out? Or someone who loves spending time with friends, but then tells us she thinks it's a waste of time that she should be spending on her career? In both of these cases, there's something wrong. In the best case, valuing brings together or harmonizes our desires, our emotions, and our thoughts about what makes our lives go well.

Values are also ultimate rather than instrumental. What I mean by this is that the things we identify as our values—things like friendship, security, meaningful work, compassion—are likely to be things that we want for their own sakes rather than purely for the sake of something else. I do love that my husband takes out the garbage and fixes flat tires on my bicycle, but I don't just value our relationship as a means to trash management and bike maintenance. If you value your family, it's not just because they call on your birthday or cook you Thanksgiving dinner: some of your desires, emotions, and beliefs about their importance are directed specifically at them, not at what they can do for you.

So, values are ultimate goals that harmonize our desires, emotions, and thoughts. Because values are important and integrated into our psychology, they tend to be fairly stable. This doesn't mean that we can never change them, but they aren't fleeting. This makes sense, because most of our values require some commitment to get what's good out of them. It takes some time and effort to achieve a great friendship, for example. And many valued activities such as music, sports, or art require developing our skills in order to appreciate their true value.

It is worth noticing that there isn't always a clear line between our ultimate values and our instrumental goals—it's more like a continuum—but we can identify some paradigm cases on each side. Shopping goals are instrumental. We don't usually want shoes for their own sake: we want them in order to look good, to fit in, to make an impression, to be comfortable, or to dance without injury. The goal of making a lot of money is also a paradigmatically instrumental goal. Unless you've got some kind of disorder, you don't want to accumulate hundred-dollar bills; rather, the point of money is what it can buy. On the other side of the continuum, relationships with loved ones are paradigmatically ultimate values. People don't value their children because of what their children can do for them; they value them for their own sakes. Health is in the middle. Some people care about health merely instrumentally: they want to be healthy so that they can do other things. But many people value health for its own sake in addition to caring about what it allows them to do.

Even if there aren't clear lines, there is some system. Think of all of your goals, from the most significant values to the most trivial whims, as forming a kind of web or network. Some of the strands are very strong and hold other parts of the web together. For many people, family is a value like this: it includes desires, emotions, and thoughts, and it gives meaning to many of the other things we do. If you ripped out one of these major strands, many other things would be disturbed. If I stopped caring about my family, so many things would have to change in my life that I would barely recognize myself at the end. Other strands are wispy and not connected to much. My desire for shoes to wear to a wedding is like this—it's a little bit connected to my desire not to have sore feet and my desire to look nice, but it wouldn't disrupt very much in my life to just give up on finding new shoes.

If you find the web metaphor helpful, you can think about the quest to understand what matters as a quest to understand your web of values, goals, desires, emotions, and thoughts: what the strands are like, what holds them together, what threatens their cohesion. Since different metaphors click with different people, for those of you with green thumbs, think of it as a quest to learn about your garden: what plants you have, how they fit together aesthetically and botanically, and what threatens to turn your garden into a field of weeds.

Values, then, are relatively stable, important, ultimate goals that include our desires, emotions, and thoughts. Because of that, they organize how we live our lives, give us a sense of who we are, and are what we think about when we reflect on the state of our lives. If you pause to think about whether your life is going well or badly, you are likely to find yourself thinking about the different things you care most deeply about: "Well, my children are healthy and I love my job, so things are going pretty well," or "My job is killing me, but I still have my health and friends who love me, so all things considered, my life is OK." These familiar assessments appeal to values—family, work, health, and friendship—as the standards for how things are going.

ARE THESE THE RIGHT VALUES?

Now that we know what values are, we can ask again: why do they matter? The easy answer is that they "just do." As I have defined them, values simply *are* goals that matter to us. But that answer raises a deeper philosophical question: how do we know if what matters to us actually matters? How do we know if we have the right values? Shouldn't we start with what is, in fact, *good*, rather than starting with what we happen to value? Indeed, isn't that what philosophers are supposed to tell us?

To answer this challenge, let me ask another question: if I told you what matters, would you believe me? If I said, "What really matters is devoting your life to teaching philosophy" or "The most valuable things in life are a long-lasting marriage and canine companions," those of you who have done other things with your lives than what I've done with mine would be quite within your rights to say "no thanks." These values are too specialized to be the answer for everyone. On the other hand, if I said, "What matters in life is proving that you are better than everyone else" or "the most valuable thing in life is amassing as much money as you can for yourself," almost nobody would believe me. The problem with these answers is not that they are too specialized, but that they're totally misguided. What kind of answer could I give you that you would accept? It would have to be one that makes sense to you, which means—surprise!—it would have to fit the values you already have.

There's a 1983 Monty Python movie about the meaning of life (it's called *The Meaning of Life*) in which Michael Palin opens the envelope that contains the answer to the movie's question and informs the viewers: "Well it's nothing very special. Try to be nice to people, avoid eating fat, read a good book every now and then, get some walking in, and try and live together in peace and harmony with people of all creeds and nations." One thing that's funny about this is that it really isn't very special, and yet there is also something profound about it. Be nice to people, watch out for your health, do some enjoyable and interesting things, and live in peace and harmony. What else would a good life be?

The point here is that there is no place to start except with what matters to us. I can't persuade you of some kooky new theory of the good life that is totally disconnected from what already matters to you. If I recommend something you think is meaningless or bad, you aren't going to believe me when I tell you it's good. We have to start with our concerns, our cares, our *values*. But this does not mean that whatever you happen to think about what matters is exactly right. We have to start from where we are, but we can make improvements from there.

The question of whether we have the right values really has two versions. One question is whether the values we have match some objective, universal values such as the moral values of justice, human dignity, or the greatest happiness. This is an important philosophical question, to be sure, but it is not really the topic of this book.

The other question is whether we have the right values *for us*, given our circumstances and personalities. This question *is* the topic of this book. As we'll see, it's not necessarily the case that whatever goals and values you happen to have are the ones that are best in this sense. We're unlikely to be completely wrong about family, work, health, and friendship, but these basic, general values are understood and prioritized in many different ways. We can improve on what we take the successful pursuit of our values to be, how we decide to pursue them, and how we prioritize them with respect to each other. Indeed, we *must* do this, and we are pushed to do it when we encounter conflicts.

Notice that we already have a clue about what it means for there to be better and worse values in this second sense (better *for us*). First, some values have greater psychic harmony—they are more integrated into our personalities and a better fit with our human nature. These values are better for us because inner conflict is an obstacle to fulfillment. Second, some values fit better together. Better values and goals are those that we can actually realize together in some satisfying way.

Of course, it's possible that some people, starting where they are, will not be able to arrive at good places for themselves. We'll consider this possibility later in the book when we talk about radical change. It's also possible that some people, given their starting points, will arrive at a very bad place from the point of view of that first question about moral values. Though this isn't the main topic of the book, we will get to the question of moral values in chapter 8.

For now, let's put these worries aside and turn our attention to how we can adjust our goals and resolve our conflicts in ways that make our own lives better. To begin, we need to know what our values and goals are.

3

WHAT ARE OUR VALUES . . . AND WHAT SHOULD THEY BE?

We all know what our values are, don't we? I have already been talking as if my own values are quite obvious and settled: family, friendship, philosophy, being a nice person, health, and happiness. And yet, so much great literature, as well as a wave of recent psychological research, suggests that we probably don't know our own values and goals as well as we think we do.[1] Consider how long it took for Elizabeth Bennet to realize that she loves Mr. Darcy in Jane Austen's *Pride and Prejudice*. "How despicably I have acted!" she cries, not long after harshly rejecting his marriage proposal. "I, who have prided myself on my discernment . . . How humiliating is this discovery! . . . Till this moment I never knew myself."[2] Only once Mr. Darcy is gone does she realize that her relationship with him is exactly the match of intellectual equals she has wanted.

Despite our general confidence that we know what we value, I would guess that this kind of experience is familiar to most readers. We can be surprised to learn how much something means to us when it is taken away. ("You don't know what you've got 'til it's gone," as the song goes.[3]) This wouldn't ring true if we were always perfectly informed about our own values. There is a sense in which we know what matters to us, in the vague and general terms that might appear on a "what are your values?" survey. But there's another sense in which we often discover that we have been mistaken or ignorant: we don't always know exactly what matters, in what way, or how much.

One explanation for this is something we've already talked about: the omnipresence of hidden goals. There are states of affairs that our brains represent as desirable, and that our bodies are inclined to pursue, even if they aren't the focus of our conscious attention at the moment. The flashlight of our attention can't shine on all of our goals at once. It's also true that people differ in terms of awareness of their goals. People who have been in counseling or career coaching may have a very clear idea, while others who haven't thought about it much may have only a vague sense. This chapter is addressed to both types of people. If you're already very reflective about your goals, you probably know that it's an ongoing process. If you're not like that, it's likely that you have nevertheless experienced the consequences of value conflicts and (I hope) will see the benefit of working through those conflicts by identifying what matters most to you.

None of us (even those of us who have a penchant for reflection) has a detailed set of well-defined values sitting around in our brains waiting to be discovered. Rather, we muddle through life with a general sense of the things we care most about and a vague idea of what it means to succeed. Our undefined, general values—work, family, friendship, art, creativity, sports, and so on—are open to interpretation. What kind of work? Family in what sense? Friendship with whom? Music appreciation or music performance? Team sports or individual sports? Creativity in what? We can answer these questions in ways that make it easier or more difficult to succeed. As I said in the "Roadmap," the process of getting more specific about what matters, in what way, and how much, is a process of both understanding and improvement.

Why do we need a better understanding of our values and goals? Why not just muddle along? That may work to some extent, until we have a conflict of goals, a crisis, or a problem. When we confront challenges, getting more specific will help us.[4] If we do it well, we can see what's at stake in our choices. Once we recognize that, we can refine our goals and values in ways that will promote greater fulfillment. So, how do we do this? Here are some suggestions:

Five strategies for understanding and improving your values and goals

1. Introspection
2. The lab rat strategy
3. Guided reflection
4. Learning from others
5. Exploration

Before we dive in, I want to preempt a possible misunderstanding of this process. Figuring out what matters to you is not just self-absorbed navel gazing. As you think about what matters to you and why, you have to think not just about yourself, but also about the values themselves. For example, if I reflect on what the value of "work" means to me, I will think about *what the work is like* and what it actually accomplishes. This point is most obvious in the fifth strategy we'll discuss below, but even in simple introspection, our insights about what we value will be informed by our thoughts about the values themselves. In addition, we can't figure out what matters just by thinking about it. We need to do things, to feel, to react, to learn from experience. If we sit around thinking all the time, we won't have the right inputs to our reflection.

INTROSPECTION

The most basic form of introspection requires you to simply ask yourself: what do I value? This isn't a bad place to start and we can supplement it with some thought experiments. For example, you could try thinking about what you'd grab from your home if it were on fire and you had to get out fast. Assuming my husband could get out on his own, I'd take the dogs, my laptop, old family photo albums, and some jewelry that belonged to my grandmother. Once you've taken care of the living creatures in your home, this way of thinking prioritizes material (and small) things, because that's what we can carry. Notice, though, that they are probably material things with special aesthetic value or connections to something more meaningful than the object itself. My laptop has all my work on it; the photo albums and my grandmother's jewelry represent connections to family and friends. So, there may be some insight to gain here.

A better thought experiment for directing us to our values might be to think about what we would prioritize if we had to move from our homes and had the luxury to choose where to go. What are the things you would think about if you had to leave your current home and live somewhere else? When I have actually been in this position, I have thought about whether I would be near friends and family in the new place, what the politics were like, what work would be like, opportunities for hiking, biking, and walking, and generally whether I believed I would be happy there. This actually does fairly well at representing my values. In fact, most people's lists of values include family, friendship, health, work, and happiness. Faith, music, sports, and volunteering will be on many lists, too.

These are all examples of things we value doing, having, or pursuing. We also value ways of *being*. Most of us value honesty and kindness, or maybe just "being a good person." People also value qualities such as spontaneity, creativity, integrity, resilience, or being a fun person. The right thought experiment here might be to think about what qualities you'd want to preserve if your consciousness were going to be transported into another body! If I were told that a consciousness transplant was my only path to survival, what existing personality traits would I be most concerned about? Or what would I change if there happened to be a transporter setting for that? Personally, I would want to make sure the new me had integrity and a sense of humor. I wouldn't mind if the transporter chief could edit out my tendency to be anxious about trivial things.

We can make some progress with such thought experiments, but introspection is a limited strategy. One problem is the massive amount of stuff (emotions, memories, thoughts, desires, and so on) that is out of reach of our working memory when we sit down to think. This problem is compounded by biases and self-protective habits that interfere with our acknowledging the facts when we run across them.[5] We can see this problem even in the easy shopping case. I like to see myself as someone who doesn't care more about how I look than I do about the health of my feet. But past shoe purchases indicate that this may not be totally accurate. I have bought uncomfortable shoes because they're cute and on sale, and sometimes, let's face it, just because they're cute. If I just introspect—"what are my shoe priorities?"—I find comfort at the top of the list. Introspection may do a better job telling me about the person I want to be than the person I am.

Let's take another example. I have always told myself that I am not a competitive person. Indeed, I am less competitive than my husband, which makes it easier to see myself as someone who doesn't care whether I win or lose a game. I once folded a great hand in a poker game to let someone win, because he was just learning the game and I felt bad for him. I generally avoid competitive games; I prefer solitary sports to team sports. All of these things went into my story about myself as someone who doesn't care about winning. Recently, however, I've had a few experiences that made me doubt this story. The most obvious was when I was at the house of some new friends who suggested playing a game. "Sure," I said, "But I'm not very competitive," and they both burst out laughing. Clearly, they thought I was joking. This and a few similar experiences made me reinterpret some of my story. Maybe I avoid competitive games not because I don't like them, but because I don't like losing. Maybe the reason I haven't stopped talking about letting that guy win at poker twenty-five years ago is that I actually *did* care that I lost the hand.

Introspection really only reveals the tip of the iceberg, and my competitiveness was buried by the things I told myself and my desire to see myself a certain way. So, there are at least two problems with this practice: there's too much stuff that is not available to conscious attention and we have self-protective habits that interfere with acknowledging the facts.

If introspection is limited in these ways, what can we do aside from just reflecting on our values?

THE LAB RAT STRATEGY

If we wanted to know about the goal hierarchies of an animal, we would observe its behavior and its reactions to its environment, and we would think about what we know about its nature (how it evolved, for example). If you have pets, you're probably familiar with this mode of investigation. Is your dog happy? Well, is she enjoying her food and excited to go on walks? Is she cowering and having accidents in the house? From what you know of the needs of dogs, are her needs being met? Human beings have more complicated goal hierarchies than dogs, but we are still animals and we did evolve to have certain needs. This can be a useful perspective to take.

If we were studying rats, the first thing we would want to know is some general information about what rats are like: their basic needs, interests, and abilities. This isn't a bad place to start when our subject is ourselves, either. Some goals are so basic to human beings that most of us just can't avoid them; they become thick strands in the web before we are old enough to think about our values. We learn our most basic values from experience. How do we learn that it's good for us to be fed and warm? We eat and feel good; we are warm and we like it. We see Mom or Dad and we feel happy. These are our earliest experiences with values. Remember that valuing something is in part wanting it and feeling positively about it. So, when we learn what produces these good feelings, we are shaping our values. As babies, we learn that security is good: being snug, dry, and having a full belly are good things. We learn that certain other people are very nice to have around, too. Not only do they bring us things we want, but they are themselves warm and comforting. We also learn that exploration is cool: it's very pleasant to reach for things and put new stuff in our mouths. As we start doing more and more things, we experience the joy of acting on our own and doing things successfully. What a thrilling moment when you can actually reach the mobile above your crib! Before we can think about values, our web of values is being constructed with affiliation, autonomy, competence, security, and exploration as some basic strands.

The idea of basic human needs will make some people think of Maslow's hierarchy of needs.[6] Abraham Maslow was an American psychologist who posited a set of needs ranging from physiological needs for air, water, and food to the more highfalutin "self-actualization" needs for achieving one's full potential. In the middle, Maslow posited needs for safety, belonging, and esteem. His idea was that we humans must have our lower-level needs satisfied before we can think about satisfying those at the higher level. This makes sense: you can't think about reaching your full potential if you are dying of thirst. This point is really important when we're thinking about how to help other people. People who are struggling to feed themselves and their children, or to find safe housing, are suffering in ways that a just and compassionate society ought to fix. When we're trying to figure out our own values, however, I'm not sure how useful it is to think about Maslow's hierarchy. For myself, I find that my values span the hierarchy and that lower-level goals are mixed up with higher-level ones. For example, my friendships and family relationships (mid-level) provide me with a sense of security (lower-level) and also allow me to realize my full potential as a good friend or caring daughter (highest-level).

I do think it's useful to think about the needs we evolved to have. It points us to goals we almost certainly have whether we recognize it or not. Many psychologists who research well-being and happiness propose lists of basic human needs that include relationships, autonomy, competence, security, exploration, vitality, and pleasure.[7] These needs are "basic" not in the sense that they are at the bottom of a hierarchy, but rather in the sense that they are persistent and more or less universal. And if we think about our development from the point of view of the evolution of goal-seeking creatures, as we discussed in chapter 2, this makes sense. Self-regulating, goal-seeking creatures like us will have some *basic psychological motivations* to explore the world, to find safety, and to affiliate with others. It makes sense that we would have a basic need for autonomy, which is the ability to direct our own lives. Autonomy allows us to explore the world and determine the actions that will help us meet our goals. It also makes sense that we have a need for competence, understood as the skills required to do what we want to do. In short, there's a lot of overlap and agreement about our basic human needs and motivations.

As we grow into reflective adults, these basic motivations take more specific shape. We add a layer of judgment to the process so that the things we want and love also become the things we choose, plan for, and believe are good for us. The need to explore becomes an interest in learning a new language. The need for security becomes a desire to have a house and a garden. The need for affiliation becomes love of friends, and so on.

So, we can learn something about our systems of values by understanding ourselves as human beings. Not only does taking this perspective help us identify our values, but it also helps us recognize conflicts and see what might be missing. Serious conflicts arise when we have goals that frustrate these strong, enduring human desires for being in relationships, making our own decisions, using our skills, learning new things, feeling good, and so on. Acknowledging the innate importance of relationships, for example, is useful for seeing what is at stake in the decision to take a job that trades higher pay for proximity to friends. And understanding the basic human need for novelty and exploration gives us a useful perspective on the costs of staying cooped up in our houses for months on end.

The appeal to our human nature, as useful as it is, isn't sufficient, though. This is because each of us interprets these broad and general values given by our human nature in different ways. So, the second thing we'll want to know when we study ourselves like lab rats is the ways in which each of us is unique. What shape do these basic human needs take in *your* life or mine? In what way do *you* care about relationships? Abstract values like "relationships" are accompanied by much more specific values that give meaning to the abstraction. Valuing friendship means valuing some specific friends. Valuing family means valuing your relationships with some specific people. Valuing success means valuing success at some specific activity. We have to get specific in order to know how to act in ways that will allow us to succeed in terms of our values. We also need to know how we prioritize the various values we have. We need to know what kinds of hidden goals and motives are working away in the background. We need to know where the conflicts are. We need to know more about ourselves than the fact that we're human.

To see how individual lab rats differ from each other, we have to observe their behavior and see how each one responds to its environment. We can use this method on ourselves. We can try to take an outside perspective and notice how we react to the way we are currently pursuing our values. In my own experience, when I have been the most stressed by conflicts in my life, my body responds by catching colds, exhibiting acid reflux symptoms, and producing headaches. This is a known phenomenon: stress causes physical illness.[8] Stress can also cause "negative mystery moods" (one of the best phrases I have learned from reading psychological research), which can clue us in to dysfunctional hidden goals.[9] Basically, stress makes you feel bummed out, a sign that your goals are not working for you. Burnout is another way that experience tells us something is amiss in our web of values. Feeling burned out is often evidence that we are putting too much of our energy into one goal—often work, childcare, or eldercare—and ignoring everything else. If you interpret your values in ways that aren't sustainable, that don't suit your personality, or that aren't compatible with your other commitments, you may burn out, even if you don't get physically ill.

Illness and burnout are two ways that reality intrudes to tell us that our values aren't working for us. Boredom and flow are two others. One of the things I've learned from advising college students is to pay attention to boredom. This unpleasant emotion is associated with an inability to focus and a lack of interest. If you're doing something that consistently makes your mind wander, or your eyes close, it's probably not where your passion lies. Of course, most of us have to do some things we find boring, but if we are trying to identify what we really value, boredom is a good clue that we haven't found it yet.

I think boredom is important evidence about our web of values and their fulfillment. Boredom makes it more difficult to fulfill our goals because it is quintessentially unmotivating. To take a fairly trivial example, think about the last book you found boring. I'm someone who has always thought (at least until very recently) that you should finish any book you start, so I have read a lot of dull books. It takes me forever to finish them and prevents me from reading other books that I would enjoy more. Boredom also shakes our confidence about our values because it does not contribute to a good narrative about why what we value actually matters. For many of the things we do, "I enjoy it" is a sufficient answer to the question of why it's a good thing to do. Why do you bake, garden, do crossword puzzles, pickle vegetables, play pool, run 10K races? Enjoyment, engagement, and fun are good answers. "Because they are boring" is no answer at all.

In defense of boredom, some researchers have argued that it has important benefits. Indeed, a recent article in a popular psychology magazine urges its readers to "embrace boredom."[10] Boredom, the article suggests, creates space for creative daydreaming and motivates us to pursue new goals. I agree that the sensation has some benefits, but I also think that if we look more closely, "embrace boredom" isn't the right advice. This is because I take it that the arguments in favor of boredom are referring to its *instrumental* value, not to the value it has *for its own sake*. It's definitely true that boring activities can have instrumental value. Reading boring books has sometimes been the only way for me to learn something I didn't know. And grading first year exams, though boring, is instrumental to understanding what my students are learning (and to keeping my job). But this doesn't mean that the experience of boredom is good in itself. It is not. If boredom makes space for creativity, it is the creativity that is good, not the boredom. If boredom motivates us to find new goals, it is *because it is aversive*. We don't like it, so we look for something that isn't boring.

Perhaps we should embrace boredom because it gives our minds a break from information overload and thereby improves our mental health. Putting away our phones for a few minutes and experiencing life without constant stimulation is probably good for us, but (again) it isn't boredom itself that is good for us. We may experience boredom when we put away our devices because we are used to distraction and we haven't cultivated any skills of mindful attention. But the point here is to tolerate boredom so that we can achieve a more serene, peaceful state of mind in the long term. Tranquility—the peaceful state of mind, or what the Ancient Stoics called "ataraxia"—is pleasant, unlike boredom. If boredom didn't lead to these other goods (creativity, new goals, serenity) it would just be a pain. So, if you find some activity boring, unless it has something else going for it, it's not a good candidate for an ultimate value. The right advice about boredom isn't "embrace boredom," but rather, "learn from boredom."[11]

Feelings of flow provide evidence on the other side. Flow is the experience of being so absorbed in some activity that you lose track of time. It is the state you are in "when fully engaged in an activity, typically a challenging activity performed well . . . It is roughly the opposite of boredom" and, according to experts in philosophy and psychology, it is an important component of psychological happiness.[12] If you have trouble recalling what causes flow for you, one suggestion from psychologists is to think about what activity you would not prefer to start if you knew that you had to stop and be somewhere else in thirty minutes.[13] For me, writing is often like this. I want long stretches of uninterrupted time to get lost in it and feel the flow. Responding to administrative emails, on the other hand, is something I'm happy to try to sneak in between a dentist appointment and a nap.

Flow is neat, but we can't be in flow all the time—we would forget to eat! So, we shouldn't forget the importance of other positive emotions, such as joy or the pleasant peace of mind (tranquility) that might *eventually* result from allowing yourself to be bored.[14] All of these positive emotions are good cues about our best values for the same reason. If certain activities typically give you experiences of flow, joy, or tranquility, you know that these activities are good candidates for the best values. This is in part because we value our own happiness, and these emotions are part of happiness. In other words, good feelings feel good, and we want to feel good! But it is also because positive emotions are some of the building blocks from which our best values are made. Our overall goal is to find values that bring our desires, emotions, and thoughts into harmony. We're looking for values that don't create conflict with our emotions, so we should pay attention to what brings us flow, joy, tranquility, and other positive emotions.

Observing yourself as if you were a lab rat is a good strategy for finding out how you are wired emotionally, which is useful information for figuring out your best values. This is especially true if some of your emotions and motivations are not completely in line with your explicit self-conception. You may like to think of yourself as a highbrow appreciator of great literature, but if you find yourself snoozing when you read Dostoyevsky and full of delight when you read romance novels, you may need to think about what your love of literature really means. More generally, your vague sense that appreciating art is very important can be given better shape once you understand what you actually enjoy.

This is a good place to observe that there can be too much deliberate reflection. To see what the rat will do, you have to let it go. To see how you're wired emotionally—especially if it's at odds with your beliefs about yourself—you need to make space for those emotions and motivations to emerge. If you're always in self-examination mode, you'll inhibit what there is to be examined.

GUIDED REFLECTION

The second alternative to simple introspection is a strategy that comes from goal pursuit psychology. It's particularly useful for uncovering the hidden emotions and motivations we just talked about. Psychologists who study goal pursuit have found that people often have conscious and nonconscious motives that aren't well aligned. To strengthen alignment, they suggest using our imagination to envision our ideal futures. The idea is that imagination is more in touch with our hidden motivations, because it doesn't require that we articulate our goals in explicit language. We can give these imagination exercises some structure. Instead of just fantasizing about "your ideal future" in general, you can prompt yourself with specific cues such as questions about what activities you like, what kind of relationships you would like to have, or in what direction you would like your career to go. You can prompt yourself with questions about what qualities you admire in others, what skills you would like to acquire, or what your ideal family life would look like.[15]

Of course, these questions could have explicit verbal answers that you might access by simple introspection, but you can also use them to spark imagination. You can tell your reflective, problem-solving mind to relax and try to envision ideals that aren't meant to be practical. Or you can put the questions in mind before you go to sleep, or take a walk, or relax in the bath, and then see what comes to you when you're not deliberately thinking about them. I once worked with a career coach who took me through an imagination exercise that ended with my looking up to see a billboard with my name on it. What was on the billboard, she asked? My answer: a bright blue sky with a big happy-face emoji and the headline *Tiberius Writes Groundbreaking Book on Well-Being!* What did I learn from this? I learned, for one thing, that my imagination is artistically unsophisticated—the blue sky and yellow happy face was such a cliché! But, more importantly, I learned how much I love writing and contributing to the world of ideas. This was at a time when most of my energy was going into administration, so it was important to be reminded of what I actually value about my job. The point of the exercise was to get the hyperverbal, conscious me—the one who chose the administrative position—out of the way of my underlying passions.

Turning to our imaginations in these ways should increase our awareness of our goals—even to some extent, those that were previously hidden. It can therefore help us improve our values, because our best values are the goals that harmonize with our conscious and nonconscious motives.

LEARNING FROM OTHERS

A third strategy is learning about our values and goals from others. We're all familiar with people who will tell you when you have spinach in your teeth. Many of us are also lucky enough to have friends we can rely on to tell us when we're doing something that's making us miserable or missing out on something that could make us happy.

We can't learn everything from our own experience. This is so obvious when it comes to learning about the world that it hardly bears mentioning. Most of what I know about the world I know because I've heard it from reliable sources. A similar point is true about valuing. As children, we learn from parents and teachers about all sorts of new, fun activities—kids couldn't finger-paint, knit, take gymnastics, swim, or bake without the help of adults. We also learn why it's good to be polite and to treat our siblings fairly. As adults, we learn from other travelers what it would be like to visit a certain country, from athletes how difficult it is to play a particular sport, from music teachers how much we'd have to practice to play the piano decently, and so on. We learn what to value from these people's experience because it helps us to discover what we do and do not desire, what we do and do not find enjoyable, exciting, or peaceful, and what we are able to endorse in our plans. We would be very limited in our options if we could learn only from our own experience; we need to learn from others to find the values that are best for us.

What may be less obvious than this is that we can also learn about *ourselves* from others. We can pay attention to other people's reactions to the things we say and do. Sometimes these come in the form of explicit observations and advice, as

47

was the case with my friend who pointed out that I was pay-ing more attention to men than to women. Sometimes they are reactions that aren't intended to inform you of anything, as was the case with the friends who burst out laughing when I said I was not competitive. We can also learn about the forces that shape our sense of things. Our friends can give us a different perspective on how we see ourselves.

Simine Vazire, a psychologist who has studied self-knowledge extensively, argues that there are some things about ourselves that we are pretty good at discovering and certain things that other people see more accurately than we do.[16] In particular, Vazire shows that we are better at recog-nizing more internal things, such as our level of self-esteem, whereas other people are more accurate about our qualities that have external standards, such as intelligence. Vazire uses an ingenious method to study these phenomena. She uses a tool called the electronically activated recorder (EAR), which records what subjects actually say as they go about their daily lives. These recordings are coded for the qualities of interest in the research (self-esteem and arrogance, for instance) and then compared to self-reports and peer reports about the per-son. If you just ask someone what they're like, their answer may be distorted by their desire to make a certain impression; people are not the most reliable reporters about their own character. The EAR tool is a very clever way of getting around the problem. For our purposes, what's interesting about this research is that it provides evidence that other people are good sources of information about some things that are relevant to our self-knowledge, but not others. In my case, whether I pay more attention to men speaking than women speaking is a matter of fact that others are probably better able to see. Where

I get my flow experiences, on the other hand, is likely something I have to discover for myself.

Learning about ourselves from others is not easy, of course. If Vazire is right, there are things about us that other people just don't have very good access to. And there are other pitfalls. One is that people have ulterior motives. Sometimes friends, lovers, or family members see us as they do because of their own needs, biases, and blind spots. My husband is always telling me that I'm *not* competitive, but I think that's largely because I'm not *as compared to him*. A partner who is dependent on you financially may be unable to help you explore how much you really value your lucrative job. Your parents may be so stuck on seeing you as their little girl or boy that they do not recognize the ways you have changed. A supervisor who wants to keep his employee as his underpaid assistant might be motivated to advise her that she wouldn't enjoy taking MBA classes in night school.

We need to look for self-knowledge in the right places. This can be challenging. Sometimes it's obvious whose opinions we should discount, but often it isn't. People who want to manipulate us are usually pretty good at hiding their ulterior motives, or at convincing us that they have our best interests at heart. For someone like me, who is naturally inclined to care too much what others think, there's a real risk of looking for approval in all the wrong places. When I was in college, I dated someone who was particularly skilled at making me think that his interests were my interests. The wake-up call for me was seeing a movie together and finding myself unable to tell if I liked it or not until I heard what he thought about it. I cringe when I think of this, but, as I said, he was a skilled manipulator. My concern for his opinion (reinforced by his

pattern of getting angry when I disagreed with him) so domi-
nated the experience of watching the movie that it crowded
out everything else.

One pernicious force that causes people to look for information and approval in the wrong places is internalized oppression, what happens when people in a disadvantaged group
come to accept the norms that keep them down. It has the
potential to profoundly distort their sense of whose opinion
matters. One of the most poignant and succinct descriptions
of internalized oppression (in this case, racism) comes from
Martin Luther King Jr.'s 1963 "Letter from Birmingham Jail,"
in which he describes

> when you suddenly find your tongue twisted and your
> speech stammering as you seek to explain to your six-year-
> old daughter why she cannot go to the public amusement
> park that has just been advertised on television, and see
> tears welling up in her little eyes when she is told that
> Funtown is closed to colored children, and see the de-
> pressing clouds of inferiority begin to form in her little
> mental sky.[17]

More recently, and even more briefly, Ibram X. Kendi put it
this way: "Racist ideas make people of color think less of themselves, which makes them more vulnerable to racist ideas."[18]
A person who believes in her own inferiority is at risk of paying too much attention to the opinions of the wrong people
because, to her, many others will appear to be more authorita-
tive. If you believe you should be in an inferior position, you
may be inclined to defer to people in a superior position and
to look to them for confirmation. (Of course, this is not the
only problem caused by internalized oppression.)

Because our values are not perfectly clear and well-defined, other people can influence how we interpret our values and goals. For example, think about women who find themselves doing a lot of emotional labor: stressing about how to present bad news so as not to enflame interpersonal conflicts or step on fragile egos, for example. Women in such positions often look for the approval of the very people who benefit from their care and time. Male colleagues will heap approval on women who are nurturing and unassertive, and this can look like confirmation of women's caring values. But do women really value deference and caring for others in this particular way? Or do we value something like helpfulness that could be thought of in a different way, a way that didn't cause us to sacrifice so much of our time (and possibly our self-respect)?

Unfortunately, there's probably no easy way to know which people to trust and which not to. Indeed, deciding whom to trust is part of the complex process of figuring out what matters. That said, although there's no neat "how-to" guide to inform us, there are some rules of thumb. We should try to keep our own most steadfast and reliable values in mind. We can think about what others stand to gain by trying to influence our values. Crucially, we should ignore the opinions of those who want us to serve them or who think we are inferior; these are not people who can help us figure out what values are best for us. We can also look around for second and third opinions when we're not sure. Triangulating among different friends and thinking about what ulterior motives, blind spots, and biases people are likely to have can be helpful. A diversity of opinions is often illuminating. We can also rely on the other strategies we've talked about in this chapter: paying attention to our own feelings, pleasures, and pains and using our imaginations to get below the surface of our conscious self-conception.

Despite the risks of learning from others, as long as we follow these rules of thumb we are probably better off being open to learning from others than suppressing our social nature and trying to become invulnerable loners. There's a risk of trying to learn from the wrong people, but the flip side to this warning is that we may find people who are excellent teachers. A friend who does have your best interests at heart, and who knows you well enough to see how you engage with your own values from the outside, can be extremely helpful. Most women I know have friends like this. The friend who observes that you're miserable when you're reading Russian novels, which you committed yourself to do for the sake of some misguided sense of literary achievement. The friend who points out the number of times you've said you'd like to do something creative and finds a watercolor painting class you could take. The friend who can remind you why you quit your job when you're feeling insecure about changing careers. These friends are worth their weight in gold, and we would do well to make room for what we can learn from them about our values.

EXPLORATION

Even if—as I've suggested—we have to start where we are, with the values that we have, this does not mean that we shouldn't explore what else is out there. Exploration is important to the process of figuring out what matters. Insofar as our values are undefined and vague, we need to know the options for making them more specific. Let's take "family," for example. If you were raised to think that a family is two parents, 2.5

children, and a dog, you may struggle with the value if you are uninterested in pair bonding, procreating, or pets. You need to discover what else family can mean to people: how it can be valuable to us even if it doesn't look like Ward and June Cleaver. Or think about work. You may have a vague idea that your work must be your passion (rather than a way to pay the bills so you can pursue your passion elsewhere), or that work must be highly paid to be worthwhile, or that work should occupy all the time you do not spend with your children. These ideas could work for some people, but they won't work for everyone. People whose passions are for things that society doesn't reward with money may be better served taking jobs that just pay the bills, for example. Exploring the options—understanding the various ways that people value things such as family and work—helps us home in on what really matters to us about these values.

Another way that exploration is important to figuring out what matters is that there may be things it would be good for us to value that aren't currently on our radar. Millicent the turtle from chapter 2 might also like blackberries if she tried them, for instance, and I might like tap dancing. In other words, there might be things that aren't in your system of values that would suit the kind of person you are and fit well with your other values. Exploration can help us find them. Now, often these "new" values are really just versions of, or ways of getting, old values. Maybe blackberries are just a means to the value of a full belly for Millicent, and tap dancing is just a means to fitness for me. But there may be cases in which we can discover a genuinely new value.

For example, take play. I mentioned earlier that I once worked with a career coach. I did this when I took on an administrative position and was worried about not being able to manage the stress. One of the first questions she asked me was, "What do you do for play?" I honestly had no idea what she was talking about. Play? You mean, like card games? What she meant was something I did for the joy of it, not to tick off a box on my ever-expanding to-do list, not to make someone else happy, and not to improve my health. My first emotional reaction to this was a feeling of failure: "I study well-being and I'm not doing it right!" Once I got over that, I had to think about what it meant that I couldn't identify anything in my life that really fit the bill. Do humans need to play? Some philosophers think so.[19] But even if it's not a basic human need, it's probably something that my personality could use more of. This was something I had to discover.

How do we explore the world of values? Exploring the world in general is a good place to start, because we learn what has value through all of our experience. We are constantly evaluating. Importantly, we can also learn about what matters from the experience of others. We've already talked about some of the ways friends can be helpful, including by showing us the joy and interest of the things they value. And friends are not the only source of this information. Other people in general—even fictional characters—can enlarge our perspectives on what matters and allow us to reframe something old or discover something new.

Exploration doesn't pair well with deliberate reflection and introspection in the moment. You're not likely to find a new activity you enjoy if you're asking yourself, "Is this really worthwhile?" the whole time you're doing it. If I have to ask myself, "Am I playing yet?" I'm probably not quite getting it. Introspection and skeptical questions—though sometimes useful—get in the way here. Once again, we see that figuring out what matters isn't just self-examination. It requires a kind of openness to experience that is at odds with thinking too much.

PUTTING IT ALL TOGETHER

From the strategies we have considered, we gain information about our goals and values, where there are conflicts and where there is harmony, what's working and what isn't. These strategies are not always distinct and even when we use them at different times, ultimately we need to put the results together—through introspection, exploration, knowledge of human nature, observations of our emotional reactions, the results of our imaginative efforts, and other people's responses to us—and decide what it all means for what really matters to us.

I certainly had to put things together when it came to the value of play. Feeling overwhelmed and demoralized by email and lists of tasks was evidence that something was missing. So was feeling as though I was losing my capacity to find anything joyful. I also had evidence from some loved ones who told me that I was too hard on myself, and from watching the examples of other friends who seemed to be having a lot more fun than I was. All of these sources of evidence taught me that my system of values, which didn't include "play," could stand some improvement.

The self-understanding we achieve through all these methods will always be a work in progress, for a few reasons. First, most of us have systems of goals, values, and underlying motivations that resist perfect understanding; these systems are complex and elusive. It's just too hard to know it all. Second, what we're trying to understand changes as we're trying to understand it. This is in part because our circumstances change, and this influences what matters to us. Some obvious examples have to do with aging. In our twenties, thirties, and forties (if we're lucky), we do not think about taking care of our parents, because our parents don't need us. But then when we hit our fifties and sixties, many of us find ourselves suddenly with this new thing to care about: the health and welfare of our parents. Similarly, for people who are parents, being a good parent is typically a more demanding goal when your children are young than it is when they have left the nest. What you need to learn about yourself in one decade is different from what you need to know in the next.

There is another reason that our values change as we're trying to discover them. As we're trying to figure out what matters to us, we also encounter problems and conflicts. Indeed, problems and conflicts are often the reason we're motivated to think about what matters in the first place. When you face your work/life balance problem, you are prompted to consider what really matters to you about work and about "life." To resolve conflicts, we have to refine our values. This means that our values are taking shape through the process of discovering them. There is, in other words, an interaction between our attempts to understand our values and what there is to understand. And this is why figuring out what you value is not an entirely separate process from figuring out the best values for you.

Understanding what matters to us now, even if it is always a work in progress, is an important step in fulfilling our values. You can't do what matters if you don't know what it is. Knowing our values has another benefit, too. Many of us spend too much time fretting about things that don't actually matter that much. I have been known to worry intensely about whether I sent a poorly worded email and other relatively trivial things—and I read enough advice columns to know that I'm not alone in this. Knowing what matters helps us not sweat the small stuff. It can also help us avoid thinking that our lives will be vastly improved by the next shiny object, a pattern of thinking that is encouraged by our consumerist culture. If we know what really matters, we may be less inclined to fall into the trap of thinking that if we only had that car or those clothes (or that watch or those whatevers), then we would be happy.

Once we have an idea of what really matters to us, the next step is to try to live up to or realize those values in our actions— to do the things that matter to us and be the people we want to be. As we do so, we encounter conflicts. Our efforts to resolve them lead us to rethink and refine what matters to us, or how we ought to pursue it. In the next chapter we'll focus on these next steps: resolving conflicts and realizing our values in action.

4

ON STRAWBERRIES AND SAFETY
OR, HOW TO RESOLVE CONFLICTS

Once our friend Millicent the turtle understands that she wants both strawberries and safety, she has to figure out what to do, because crossing the road requires sacrificing the second. Once I have decided to order a healthy lunch, I should take the necessary steps and avoid large amounts of alcohol and saturated fat. Simple. And yet it's not quite so simple, because as soon as we start putting our goals into action we encounter conflicts. Personally, when I want a healthy lunch, I'm often forced to choose between one that has more nutrition and one that makes it easier to count carbohydrates so that I know how much insulin to take. The easiest option for insulin dosing is a prepackaged thing that comes with the carb info written on the package. This usually isn't the healthiest option in other respects. I also have limited time, so eventually my search for the perfect lunch will conflict with other important goals I have, like writing this book. We can see how unresolved conflict hurts us: if I can't come to a compromise among my subgoals, I'll never eat. At least in this simple example, I'm not internally conflicted about eating: I do want lunch of some kind or another! But when it comes to our complex hierarchies of values and goals, we can experience inner conflict, too.

To take a less simple example, once I realize that I need something called "play" in my life, I have to figure out how to get that compatibly with the other things I value. Play will conflict with spending time doing other things. My nagging, judgy sense that play is only for children will also compete with my attempts to incorporate it into my life.

We can divide the main types of serious conflict that cause trouble for us into three types: within-goal conflict, intergoal conflict, and conflict with our environment. *Within-goal conflict* occurs when our different attitudes toward our goal don't line up: when our emotions, desires, and beliefs about whatever it is are pulling in different directions. For example, we sometimes love to do things that we judge are bad for us. The person who grew up in a strict Pentecostal community that forbids dancing may find himself wanting to dance but also thinking that it's bad for him to do so. The purely hypothetical person who wants to be nice, but also thinks that her desire to be nice is the result of sexist socialization, might want to be nice and think she should be less nice at the same time. We can also think things are good for us even when those things just leave us cold. This often happens when we inherit ideas about what is valuable from our parents. I've talked to many students who arrive at college believing that they value a life as a doctor or accountant because that's what their parents taught them, and then realize that they are bored silly in their science or accounting classes. These students value work and success. But when they think about what exactly this means, and they understand "work" and "success" as "being a heart surgeon" or "being a wealthy accountant," they arrive at values that are not ideal for them. One student I recall in particular we can call Phil. Phil loved his philosophy classes but was convinced that philosophy was not a good thing to like. Philosophy was where he came alive; it's where he found himself with motivation to study and participate in class. Unsurprisingly, it's also where he was getting the best grades. But he didn't really think that these motivations were a good reason to major in philosophy and he was still in the grip of the belief that it was dumb to major in the liberal arts. This conflict between his passion and the judgments he inherited from his parents was making him really unhappy. Although he didn't see it, the conflict was also frustrating his overarching goals. You are more likely to be successful in college when you do something you're motivated to do (evidenced by Phil's excellent performance in his philosophy classes), and you're very unlikely to be successful doing work that you find incredibly boring.

To take another example, think of a man who was raised in a way that emphasized very traditional gender roles. Let's call him John. Like most of us, John values family, and when he tries to examine what this means, his understanding of the value of being a father is heavily influenced by the "stoic breadwinner." John Wayne is his namesake as well as his model for manhood. But for the John I'm imagining, this creates internal conflict, because John longs to spend more time with his kids and to be a cuddly, effusive dad. He has also become convinced (at least in theory) by enlightened arguments he has heard that men should be able to be more expressive than the old cultural stereotypes allowed. The "John Wayne" understanding of the value of parenthood is a bad fit with John's desire to be cuddly and effusive, but he has internalized it enough that he also feels embarrassed by his desires. This conflict between John's desire to be a cuddly dad and his shame about this very desire frustrates his goals. It's hard to be a good father when you don't actually know what that means and when your own feelings pull you in two different directions.

The second kind of problem, examples of which have already cropped up in this book, is *conflicts between our values*. It's easy to see the problem with the familiar case of work/life balance. Most people experience some conflict between the demands of their job and everything else (life!). A little bit of competition for our time is to be expected, but we sometimes understand the value of our work, or the things that compete with it, in ways that make this conflict intolerable. For example, if you think being a good mother means joining the PTA, hosting elaborate unicorn-themed birthday parties, and taking your kid to six different lessons in five different suburbs every week, you may find mothering to be in an unmanageable conflict with succeeding in your job. It's better to have values that do not compete with each other for time and attention to such an extreme.

Work/life balance is not the only kind of conflict that can create problems for us. Because relationships are so important, it's typically very painful when they conflict with other important values. Think of a gay man who is also a member of a conservative church that regards homosexuality as sinful.[1] This is a tragic conflict and it's easy to see how it creates a lack of fulfillment. It's difficult to be fully committed to a relationship that your community tells you is evil and it's difficult to accept a community that doesn't love you as you are. Divorce presents another example. If you learned about marriage from the movies, you would think that divorce is always caused by infidelity and that the relevant conflict is between one person's desire for a faithful partner and the other person's behavior. I know that this happens sometimes, but in the cases of divorce with which I am familiar, things are more complicated. If you have a partner who doesn't appreciate you, or who treats you like a child, then your romantic relationship can conflict with your self-respect. If you have a partner who doesn't do their share of childcare and housework, conflicts may arise between your relationship and your desire to do other things. Ideals of long-term relationship success inherited from one's family or church sometimes conflict with a person's desire to find joy, when the two people in the relationship have grown apart and no longer enjoy being with each other.

The third way we can go wrong is by pursuing *values that are a bad fit with our physical and social environments*. For example, given my type 1 diabetes and my shortsightedness, it would probably have been bad for me to value being an astronaut. Myopic, diabetic space travelers are not in high demand. Someone who lives at the Equator probably shouldn't value winter sports. Someone with a severe cat allergy would be better off not valuing fostering homeless cats.

Of course, finding a fit between our values and our environments is not always a simple matter. This is because our environments can change—and changing them can become part of what we value. If I had been born fifty years earlier, I can easily imagine someone telling me that I should not value a career in philosophy, because the road for women philosophers is as rocky as the road for diabetic astronauts. If we all curtailed our values to fit the world we were born into, we would never strive to improve the world. Women philosophers in the generation before me valued philosophy despite discouragement, and they changed things for the better in ways that benefit me now. For some of these women, changing the world became part of what they valued. We do need to pay attention to what the world allows: we can't live well if we are constantly frustrated in everything that matters to us. But this does not mean that we can only value what fits *easily* with our surroundings. We'll discuss this topic more in the next chapter, but for now let's turn to the general question of what to do about conflicts.

Once we identify our conflicts, there are some basic strategies we can use:

Three basic responses to conflict

1. Prioritizing and adjusting means to ends
2. Giving up one of the conflicting goals
3. Reinterpreting our values

Thinking again of our easy shopping case, the first strategy works well if you can do it. If you know that price is your highest priority, appearance second, and comfort third, you'll have an easier time settling on a pair of shoes. You can also adjust some of your instrumental goals: if *comfortable* shoes are pursued as a means to having shoes you can dance in, you could decide to dance barefoot and not worry about the height of the heel. Giving something up entirely may also work well. If you can sacrifice appearance, you'll vastly reduce your conflict: it shouldn't be too hard to find a pair of shoes that are cheap, comfortable, and ugly! Finally, you can reinterpret your goals to reduce conflict. For example, if you could revise your standards for attractive shoes—if you could come to see what a friend of mine calls "non-misogynist shoes" as attractive—you would have less conflict. Things get complicated when it comes to more important goals than shoes, but the basic strategies are the same.

PRIORITIZING AND ADJUSTING MEANS TO ENDS

To think through this strategy, let's turn once again to the so-called work/life balance problem. Notice that we don't typically confront this as a conflict between WORK and LIFE. Rather, we confront more specific conflicts: You are spending so much time at work that you have no time to exercise and your health is suffering. You are driving your kids to so many lessons and playdates that you're phoning it in on the job and find this very unsatisfying. You're so anxious about work that you can't be the patient, compassionate partner you would like to be. We experience conflicts between work and health, work and parenting, work and leisure, work and friendship, and so on. (Health, parenting, leisure, and friendship can conflict with each other, too, to be sure.)

To prioritize the goals that are in conflict, we need to identify which are ultimate values and which are subgoals that are more instrumental. In other words, we need to know what really matters and what only matters for the sake of something else. Sometimes prioritizing reveals easy solutions. This happens in cases where we can see that the conflict is between an ultimate value and the means to some other goal that can be easily substituted by some other means. For example, if the demands of your job conflict with going to the gym, and you only want to go to the gym for the sake of your health, there may be another path to health that doesn't cause conflict. If you can ride your bike to work, or run in your neighborhood instead of going to the gym, problem solved. The general point is that purely instrumental goals can sometimes be "swapped out," without much cost, for ones that create less conflict.

Adjusting means to ends should be a familiar strategy, because many of our goals are general enough that they can be pursued in multiple ways. If your goal is to get an education, there are many ways to do this: enroll in a university, join a reading group, take free online courses, spend time reading at a library, and so on. If your goal is to be healthy, again, there are many paths: take up running, swim, eat more vegetables, eat fewer refined foods, lift weights, and so on. You don't have to do all of these things to meet your goal; you can choose whichever way creates the least conflict. This approach of choosing means to our ends that reduces conflict is common in the domain of volunteer activities. Research on volunteering suggests that people who choose volunteer activities that fit their other goals are more effective and satisfied.[2] What's happening here is that many people have a goal of "helping others" that is very general. We want to be helpful, but we would be satisfied with many ways of doing it. In this case, it's easy to see why choosing means to the end that reduces conflict will results in more goal fulfillment. If you're an introverted person who hates talking to strangers, knocking on doors for political candidates is probably not the best opportunity for you. Unless you are working toward the goal of practicing skills you lack, you are going to be fighting your motivation to avoid doors, and you won't end up giving much of your time. When I volunteered to knock on doors for political candidates in 2012, I had a really hard time getting my conflict-averse self to do it. When I finally went out, standing at the end of the street looking at the line of houses I was supposed to approach, I actually started to cry. In 2020, I wrote letters to encourage people to vote, from the privacy of my own home, and I had much more energy for it.

We engage in this instrumental (means–end) reasoning all the time, though perhaps we don't think of it as aimed at reducing conflict. Nevertheless, that's what it does, because as long as we have more than one goal, what counts as the best means to your end is going to depend on what else you want. Spending a thousand dollars on the perfect pair of shoes would be fine if I had no other use for the money. Spending five hours a day at the gym would be fine if I had no other use for my time. But we all have multiple goals, so the best means to achieving them will be ones that make space for everything else that matters to us.

These "adjust the means" solutions are philosophically easy, because they appeal to a form of reasoning that is well understood. Instrumental reasoning is just the process of determining effective means to our ends. But the fact that these solutions are philosophically easy does not mean they are easy to find or implement. We can probably all think of times when we have kept on pursuing some goal in a way that felt as though we were hitting our heads against the wall. This seems to happen often with new goals that we're trying to introduce into our lives. For example, you want to "get in shape" and, because of an article you read in a fitness magazine that was lying around in your doctor's office, you decide that to reach this end you will become a "gym person"—five days a week for weights and cardio machines! "Gym person" is the means to your end. Unbeknownst to you, you hate the gym—the smell of it, the way it adds to your commute, the pressure to look good while sweating. But because you're busy and you haven't really thought much about why you chose "gym person," you keep trying . . . and failing. To see that you might be more successful with some other fitness activity (a team sport, running, tap-dancing classes) requires you to identify that "gym person" is a means to an end and that it isn't working for you. That isn't always easy, but identifying your different goals and values and prioritizing them so you know which one is a means and which one is the ultimate value really helps.

So far, we have talked about intergoal conflict. What about within-goal conflict? When we are internally conflicted about a goal, adjusting means to ends doesn't work, because our problem is that we haven't actually settled on an end to pursue. However, many within-goal conflicts are really undercover intergoal conflicts, and noticing this can also be very helpful. For example, think of our Pentecostal friend who loves dancing and also thinks that it's shameful and wrong. It might look as though he has a love–hate relationship with dancing itself. However, it may be that what's actually going on is a conflict between two quite different goals: the goal of experiencing joyful exhilaration and the goal of pleasing God. In this case, dancing isn't what he values: it's just a means to the end of joyful feelings. He's not internally conflicted about joy or about God; rather, joy and God are in conflict with each other. If this is the right way to describe this man's experience, then one thing he could do is take a different means to the exhilarated feeling that he loves about dancing. Perhaps skydiving would do it and perhaps God doesn't object to that. Of course, once he recognizes the conflict as such, he may also decide to give up the goal of pleasing a deity who doesn't want him to experience joy by dancing.

Prioritizing and adjusting means to ends works when we can identify ultimate goals that we can pursue in a different way without too much sacrifice. Unfortunately, life is not often this simple. Even when our subgoals are instrumental, they are often tied to other goals in ways that makes it difficult to substitute something else. Going to the gym is mainly a means to fitness, but you may be someone who really likes the social aspect of it and running by yourself doesn't give you that. When more ultimate values conflict, we can't swap out the means, so we need to do something else. We could consider giving something up.

GIVING UP GOALS

Giving up on something when faced with a conflict sounds like a good idea. And sometimes—when two goals are in direct, immediate conflict—giving one up may be the only answer. If you want to visit your parents in Florida for Thanksgiving and you also want to stay home in not-Florida, for example, you have to pick just one and abandon the other. But the "get rid of it" strategy doesn't usually work for our more ultimate values. If we think back to our illustrative turtle, Millicent's basic conflict between food and safety cannot be solved by giving up one of these ultimate values. She could give up *eating strawberries* (a specific means to the end of a full belly), but she can't give up food. Similarly, humans aren't going to abandon work, family, friendship, security, or our other most cherished values.

That said, there are some goals that are known duds. Many philosophers throughout history (from Aristotle to John Stuart Mill) have thought that being rich is a goal we should just give up. Being famous and having status are similar. What's wrong with these goals? There's nothing wrong with wanting enough money to pursue the other things you value. But this makes being rich an *instrumental* value, not an ultimate one. From the perspective of value fulfillment, one big problem is that—when these values become ultimate goals—they conflict with other important values such as relationships and feelings of happiness. There is good evidence in psychology that people who value money and status highly are likely to have lower-quality relationships, to be less satisfied with their lives, and to experience more negative emotions than people who do not.[3] (To be clear, it's not that having money makes you unhappy: the problem is caring too much about having it.)

One problem with valuing wealth, fame, and status is that these are relational goods. We have more of them when other people have less. This puts the materialistic person in competition with other people, and that's bad for their relationships. Fame is necessarily a rare commodity; we can't all be famous. "Being rich" is typically also thought of in comparative terms; people who want to be rich usually want to have more than their neighbors.[4] Striving after status causes people to go into debt in order to buy status symbols and other things to impress. Debt causes stress, which competes with the values of mental and physical health. Striving after wealth can lead people to take jobs that are remunerative but not suited to their passions, which causes more stress as well as dissatisfaction with their work life. So, wealth, fame, and status are goals it makes sense to give up or at least demote to mere instrumental status.

Addictive and self-destructive desires are also bad goals. It may seem strange to categorize them this way, because we would never list "become an addict" as one of our goals. But recall that, in the technical sense, goals are just representations in the brain of a state of affairs that attracts us and motivates us to do things, and addictive substances are represented as highly attractive. Taking lots of drugs, drinking vodka at breakfast, chain-smoking—these are goals that you would obviously be better off without. Self-destructive goals—such as the goal of not eating food, or the goal of staying with an abusive partner—are the same. We probably would not list them in our goals, but they are goals in the technical sense, and they are obvious cases of goals we should ditch.

Sometimes hidden motivations are bad for us. There is a stereotype according to which they are dark, monstrous forces that undermine our happiness. There are certainly examples like this: unacknowledged low self-esteem that causes you to sabotage relationship and career opportunities because "deep down" you don't think you deserve them, or a pathologically competitive desire to prove that you're better than everyone else, which puts other people off and causes problems at work and at home. Hidden goals like these weaken the web of values by preventing us from pursuing our ultimate values and by blocking good feelings when we do manage to fulfill them.

But not all of our hidden motivations and goals are bad. Many of them just come from our basic needs for exploration, security, autonomy, or affiliation. My hidden (from me, anyway) competitiveness isn't necessarily a bad thing: it has probably driven me to be successful in certain ways. When we are trying to identify our hidden motivations, we do well to distinguish specific desires from what I called in the last chapter our "basic psychological motivations." The former may be bad goals that we can get rid of, but we'll waste our time trying to uproot our basic human drives.

Sometimes our hidden motives stem from something really decent about ourselves, such as caring about other people's feelings. In such cases, it doesn't make sense to fight or discard our decent impulses just because they are in conflict with other goals. When people have been raised in ways that conflict with their basic interests and drives, these interests and drives often first appear as hidden motives. Think of LGBTQ people raised in hostile evangelical churches, or artists raised in families that only value security and money. For such people, recognizing and embracing nonconscious motives—bringing them out of hiding—can be the first step to changing the unfortunate values they inherited from their communities.

As a final point about hidden motives, we have to acknowledge that they can be really hard to change. One reason for this is that we're not fully aware of what they are! But even if we can get a handle on that (through therapy, or by paying attention to "negative mystery moods" or using the kind of goal-setting activities we talked about in chapter 2), they are often longstanding features of our personality. It's not impossible to change your personality, but it typically involves making small adjustments to the path, not reversing course.[5] I could make myself a less agreeable person, for sure. But I probably couldn't make myself into someone who doesn't care what other people think. Men who have been raised in traditional ways can probably change their standards of masculinity somewhat, or learn to care less than previously about whether they appear feminine, but for many men it will be hard to get rid of these things entirely.

Notice that *giving up goals* is a strategy that we can also consider for within-goal conflicts. When we find a genuine within-goal conflict, as opposed to one that is really just a disguised version of two different conflicting goals, trying to get rid of one of the competitors may be the way to go. If what the Pentecostal dancer loves about dancing—say, the feeling of sensual abandon—is exactly the same thing that God doesn't like about it, he has a genuine internal conflict. He can't both enjoy the sensuality of dancing *and* refrain from dancing to please God. One of these things has to go. We are sometimes conflicted about people in this way, as in a "love–hate" relationship. True love–hate relationships are difficult and painful. The path toward greater value fulfillment is to stop loving or hating so that you can move forward in the relationship or move on to a better one.

When we are able to identify bad goals, there are different strategies for getting rid of them or (as in the case of stubborn parts of our psyches) loosening their hold: psychotherapy, behavioral therapy, self-help books, coaching, support groups, meditation, and so on. Leaving an abusive spouse, overcoming addiction, retraining your thought patterns so you do not think you are worthless are some of the most difficult things to do in practice and I am no expert here. But once we see clearly the nature of the conflict and the right solution, these are not philosophically difficult cases. It's not hard to know what to *think*; rather, it's just really hard to follow through with action.

From the point of view of finding a way to think about conflict, the cases that are more challenging are those in which values that we cannot abandon nevertheless conflict. In such cases, we need another strategy.

REINTERPRETING OUR VALUES

Prioritizing our goals, adjusting means to ends, and getting rid of bad goals are strategies that take us a long way with many kinds of conflicts. But sometimes conflicts between more ultimate values can't be resolved in these ways. It's often not possible or desirable to give up an ultimate value. Most of us cannot give up "work" or "family," even if these are in conflict. And finding new means to our ends doesn't always solve the problem.

A third strategy comes into view when we think about the fact that many of our ultimate values are open to inter-pretation—not just about the best way to achieve them, but also what it would mean to achieve them in the first place. For example, most people who have children want to be good parents. But people don't think of what counts as a good parent in the same way. Some people think being a good mom requires baking cupcakes from scratch for every school bake sale and learning to play the violin along with their child. Some think it simply means keeping their kid fed and clothed. Similarly for friendship, some people think being a good friend means always being available for whatever help the person may need. Others think it means making time for a few hours together once a month. Still others think that a good friend is just someone it's easy to talk to no matter how long it's been since they last saw each other. There are multiple ways of thinking about what it is to be a good parent, a good friend, a good son or daughter, and so on.

We can see that there are alternative ways to understand certain key values when we look at other people. We probably all know parents of both the homemade-cupcake and the keep-'em-fed-and-clothed variety. Most of us also can observe various ways of valuing physical fitness in our circle of acquaintances. I have friends whose fitness goals are met by walking once a week and getting an annual physical, and others who are not satisfied unless they are training for triathlons. It's harder to see in our own case that we could interpret our values differently. Why is this? I think it's because the way that we think about what it means to fulfill our values influences our plans and our way of seeing the world. Our subgoals, our sense of self, our judgments about what we should and shouldn't do, our beliefs about success and failure are all woven together with the specific way we understand our values. Once you are the kind of person who believes that fitness means doing triathlons, you are probably also the kind of person who believes that walking your dog through the neighborhood doesn't count as exercise, and that continuing to improve your time is an important goal. Once you are the kind of person who takes being a good parent to require doing everything from scratch and by hand, you are also the kind of parent who thinks that buying a Hallowe'en costume at Target is failure. Goals and values form mutually reinforcing patterns that make our way of looking at things seem natural and inevitable.

In the way that I think about values—as including desires, emotions, and thoughts—this makes perfect sense. When we fully value something, our desires, emotions, and thoughts are all tied together in a way that makes it difficult to see how things could be different. And yet, we can see that other people value the same things we value in different ways. Seeing this in other people should help us realize that we can make these changes in ourselves if we have to.

And sometimes we have to. We have basic ultimate values that we can't abandon. We settle into a groove because of how we're raised, or because it suits us at the time. But the grooves we get into are not necessarily the smoothest. As we change, and as our circumstances change, we start to see conflicts. One solution is to see what it means to uphold these values in a different way. This is the strategy of reinterpretation.

Let's start with a simple example, I used to do a regular yoga class in which I had ambitious goals. I was working toward recovering my ability to do the splits and press up into a handstand, which is something that I thought looked really cool. Then I injured my shoulder and pulled a hamstring and I had to rethink yoga. I needed to think about a more abstract goal than "pressing up into a handstand," and probably also more abstract than "practicing power yoga." I needed to move to the more central values of "maintaining flexibility" or even "staying healthy" before I could see a way. Once your knees go, so do marathons, but if you see the ultimate values at stake here as "enjoying athletic competition" and "staying fit," you can focus on walking or swimming and let running go.

Aging is an equal-opportunity cause of the need to reinterpret our values. For me, aging has been a surprising process. In my youth, even into my thirties, I thought that I was on a fairly linear track of "figuring it out." I thought that when I was old, I would understand everything and coast happily through my dotage without enduring any more existential crises about what I was doing and what matters in life. It has been a bittersweet lesson to discover that this isn't how life works, at least not for me or other old(ish) people I've talked to. Instead, because our minds, bodies, and circumstances change, we have to keep on figuring things out. Sticking with the simple yoga example, I honestly believed in my thirties that I would always do power yoga and that I'd be able to do the splits in my forties. Now I'm more of a corpse pose expert. Looking around at my friends and family, I've been pretty lucky. No major surgery, no death of a close loved one, no serious illness (other than the one I've had all my life). Shit happens, as they say, and when what happens affects our values, we have to make adjustments.

These examples of physical activities are relatively straightforward. Bodies age and we have to change how we think about success or we'll always be failing. I think these examples are worth discussing, though, because they make an important point: we don't always see these necessary changes as *changes*; instead, we think of them as quitting or capitulating. Why? We don't have to see changes as capitulations, and it is often better not to. When we ask ourselves what's going well in our lives, whether we have the right goals, we have no other option but to rely on some of our values. If that's so, then it's better (all other things being equal) for us to reinterpret our values than to change them, where we can. Abandoning values destabilizes the system of goals and values we rely on. Reinterpreting gives us more stability, a better sense that we're on the right path. In other words, I'll be better off thinking, "I value my health and I'm finding new ways to maintain my flexibility as I age" than "I used to love yoga, but I've given up."

The "all other things being equal" clause is important. As we discussed in the previous section, there are some values—

like being rich and famous—that we should probably abandon if we can. Not only are being rich and famous bad for our other values, but they are also difficult to reinterpret in a way that fits our changing selves and circumstances. This has to do with the fact that the standard for "being rich" or "being famous" is set by forces outside of our control. If you live in a community in which your friends all drive Porsches, you are not rich if you can only afford a used Hyundai. You can change your standards for how much money you want from "enough to be rich" to something reasonable—enough to be comfortable, enough to take nice vacations, enough to send your kids to college—but then what you're doing is abandoning "being rich" as an ultimate value. Fame is similar. If fame is your ultimate goal, you are at the mercy of your audience; you just aren't famous if people don't know who you are.

With other values, however, we are often changing our interpretation of what we value, rather than abandoning it or failing. In the case of sports, what we are trying to do is to home in on the thing we really value about the activity and to figure out ways of continuing to get that thing despite our aging knees/shoulders/lungs/everything. Whereas, when it comes to being rich, I'm suggesting that there isn't anything about money in and of itself that we want to get; rather, what matters is what money lets us accomplish when it comes to the things that do really matter to us. In the case of fame, when we try to zero in on what is valued, I think we recognize that there's nothing about fame for its own sake that is worth wanting; rather, what's valuable is something like having our work acknowledged and rewarded. This is a reasonable value and one we can reinterpret so that we're seeking acknowledgment from people who matter, not just a bunch of random strangers on social media.

Physical activities such as sports are good examples of goals that we can reframe by identifying the values they invoke. We can change the specific sport we are attached to in response to physical changes—from power yoga to gentle stretching, from running to swimming—by finding something in the value of our sport that we can get in other ways. Or we can adapt the standards of success to our new capacities (or lack thereof). In other words, we can change how we think about what it means to be a runner, or a dancer, or a basketball player. We can adjust our mileage, our speed, and our level of competitiveness. To wean ourselves off the thrill of excellence, we can add new dimensions to our sport: join a running group so that running becomes social, take a beginner lesson in a new form of dance so that dancing becomes more mentally and less physically challenging, volunteer to referee basketball games for a local youth group so that we're helping others enjoy the sport with less risk to our ankles.

Sports are not the only example of goals we can reframe and reinterpret by appeal to values. A similar thinking process could be used with many activities. If you love the piano but are living in a studio apartment, is there a way of thinking about what you love about the piano that could be fulfilled in a different way? Do you love a certain kind of music that you could play or appreciate without a piano? Is it the skills you want to learn, and, if so, could you learn them on an electric keyboard? When our goals conflict with each other, or with the world, in ways that don't allow us to fulfill them as we have always done, we can look for what is really at stake—what we really value—that we can fulfill in a different, more harmonious way.

The strategy of reinterpretation is also helpful when it comes to work. One thing that sometimes causes a crisis for people who have been very ambitious in their jobs is the realization that they did not save the world, reinvent the wheel, or do whatever it was they thought they would do when they were in their twenties. For such people, it may be helpful to reframe career success in terms of making a contribution to a cooperative venture, rather than hanging on to a model of success that is better suited for an energetic twenty-something with all the time in the world. In my work, reinterpretation has helped with the conflict between the goal of being a successful philosopher and being a nice person. As I got older, I got sick of feeling like an imposter and became more open to positive feedback on my work from people who did appreciate it. This led me to think about both goals in a different way. Being a successful philosopher, I decided, does not have to mean publishing in journals that don't accept the kind of papers I think it is valuable to write. There are other ways to publish. Being a nice person does not have to mean never causing anyone discomfort. Sometimes people need to be made uncomfortable because what they want from you is unreasonable, and I'm not being a mean person if I assert myself.

Finding the best means to our ends isn't the only thing we can do when we reflect on our values. We also have the ability to fine-tune what our values are, and to focus on the parts of them that work best for us after all.

REALITY MATTERS

The ultimate point of all of these strategies—adjusting means to ends, prioritizing, demoting harmful goals, reinterpreting ultimate values—is, of course, to actually *fulfill* our values, to *succeed* in terms of the things that are genuinely important to us. To do this, we need to have a realistic assessment of our circumstances and of our abilities given those circumstances. Realism is built into all the strategies we have considered. The third type of conflict mentioned at the start of this chapter—conflict between our values and the environment—is always in the background as we're figuring things out. We need to understand ourselves to know which values bring us flow, we need to face the facts of aging to grasp the importance of reframing some of our ultimate values, we need to face the limits on our time to recognize the problems caused by our conflicts, and so on. To live well, we have to face the facts.

Or do we?

There is actually another option: delusion! Maybe what we are learning from our era of "alternative facts" is that we really care only about how we feel, whether or not our feelings match up with reality. Maybe when it comes to fulfilling our ultimate values, we should just care about how it looks to us, not about how it really is. There's a famous philosophical thought experiment called "the experience machine" that aims to show that, actually, we don't care only about our own feelings.[6] The experience machine is controlled by extremely trustworthy and skilled neuroscientists who program it to mimic reality perfectly, except for one thing: if you sign up to attach yourself to it, you will have more happy, pleasant experiences than you would if you continued on in your normal, real life. The philosopher who introduced this thought experiment, Robert Nozick, believes that people wouldn't sign on. He thinks that we prefer to have relationships with real people, to interact with the real world, and to accomplish real things, even if it doesn't feel as good as the fake life.

Ethics students confronting this thought experiment for the first time have all sorts of questions: What if the neuroscientists die? What if the machine breaks? How long is the contract? Can you take your girlfriend in there with you? What if you need some pain to experience real joy? But these questions generally miss the point. The fictional scenario has one sole purpose: to focus our attention on the question of whether we only care about how we feel or whether we also care about what really happens. The situation doesn't need to be very realistic to serve this purpose, so Nozick (or any ethics professor teaching this in their class) keeps modifying the thought experiment to force participants to confront this question. For example, the answer to the question about whether we need some pain to appreciate true joy is that, if this were the case, then the machine would be designed to provide as much pain as we needed to get more pleasure, because its defining feature is that it guarantees a greater total sum of good feelings.

Once my students understand the example, most of them still say they would not agree to be hooked up to it, even though they understand that it really would provide more pleasure. I think these students are the norm; most of us do care about reality, about actually doing things rather than just thinking that we are. But the students who say they would hook up have one last challenge: "How can it matter, if you can't tell the difference?" It's a feature of the machine that you wouldn't know you were in it. You would think your life was real, even though you would really be just lying in a lab connected to a big computer. The holdout students tend to say, "If you think it's real, what's the difference?" What my students need is a philosophical distinction between ontology (what is) and epistemology (what we know). From the point of view of what is, there is a very big difference between *Valerie lying in a lab believing that she is writing a book* and *Valerie sitting at her laptop writing a book*. This is true, even if I can't *know* which of these two people is actually me. The world is not limited by what we can know about it. So I can ask myself what I really care about. Do I care about writing a book? Or do I care about believing I'm writing a book? Obviously, I care about writing an actual book that other actual people can read! This makes a difference to how I will deliberate, plan, and choose. I won't choose to go to a hypnotist who could make me believe I had written a book. Instead, I'll start in on actual writing.

Thinking about virtual reality raises another problem for the delusion strategy. It's really hard to pull it off! To imagine a virtual life that is indistinguishable from real life requires a lot of suspension of disbelief and a huge dose of trust in the neuroscientists who are controlling the machine. In real life, it's not easy to intentionally employ a strategy of self-deception. For one thing, before you are successfully deluded, you have to acknowledge that you are trying to get yourself to believe false things. For another, reality tends to bite us in the bum.

One last point about the strategy of delusion and our current moment of alternative facts, fake news, and conspiracy theories. Some readers may take these phenomena as evidence that many people don't care about the facts. I don't agree. Conspiracy theories offer grand, unifying explanations that *justify* believing many falsehoods at once. If people didn't care about reality, why would they bother with these fancy theories?

It seems to me that they do care very much about reality, despite our current situation. It's just that they also have other goals that compete with their interest in reality and they manage the conflict by creating theories that they believe explain all the evidence.

Although the life of delusion may offer some pleasures, I stand by my commitment to reality when it comes to fulfilling our values. To find the right values and pursue them well, we need to understand our situation accurately.

We already discussed how to gain a more accurate self-understanding in chapter 3. Alas, the question "How do we gain accurate knowledge about the world?" is far too general to be answered by any one person. Fortunately, though, most human beings already have a lot of common sense about this. We know we should assess the evidence with an open mind and that we should have some humility about what we don't know. This is difficult to do, because we humans have a tendency to seek information that confirms what we think we know and to shun information that goes against it. This tendency is called "confirmation bias" and it seems to be at work in most of us.[7] This may be particularly true when it comes to knowledge of our own strengths and weaknesses: we like to think of ourselves as better than we are and better than average. Apparently, the vast majority of people think they are better than average at driving.[8] They can't all be right!

So, we know what to do—seek and assess the evidence with humility and an open mind—but it's not easy. The good news is that having a clear picture of our values can motivate us to use these ideas that we already have. Typically, when we understand what's important to us, we also see that whether or not we achieve it depends on the world beyond our own thoughts and feelings. That's why the strategy of delusion doesn't work for us. If you want to climb mountains in part because of the achievement, then you need to actually climb mountains, and you're better off with an accurate picture of how to get to the top. If you want to help alleviate a friend's suffering, you'll be well served by knowing some facts about the symptoms and treatments for that person's particular problem. We fulfill our values by actually living up to the standards they provide for us, not by pretending. And this provides some motivation to be realistic.

This is true even when it comes to your own personality. If what I care about is supporting women in my field, I need to listen to women. It's not enough to *think* that I listen to men and women with equal attention, if in truth I'm hanging on the words of every "philosophy bro" around and tuning out as soon as a young woman starts to speak.[9] If what I really value is being a good listener, it's not good enough for me to believe that's what I am when all my friends think I'm totally self-absorbed. If I want to be a world-class athlete or musician, I have to measure up to the standards of the world; I'm not world-class just because I feel that I am. Our values make demands! And they demand things that are beyond our control. The only way to discover whether we are living up to these demands is to look for evidence with humility and an open mind.

———

Taking stock: we've seen that living a life in which we achieve what matters engages us in a process of value identification and refinement. This involves identifying your more ultimate values, putting them into action, recognizing conflicts among your goals, reducing those conflicts by finding new means to reach your goals, and eliminating bad goals or reinterpreting what they really mean. We should keep in mind our full range of ultimate values, which will likely include health, autonomy, security, and relationships with other people. But we should also have a realistic appraisal of our circumstances and what they mean for our ability to fulfill our values.

5

VALUES IN AN UNFAIR CULTURE

Two hundred years ago, my being a woman would almost certainly have prevented me from teaching philosophy at a university. I would also have died young from diabetes, which would have significantly affected the pursuits of my values. Throughout history and at this moment, I could not climb Mount Everest in my bare feet and I could not parasail off the cliffs of Dover. These barriers are not all the same. Women were long excluded from philosophy because of the social world and its sexist norms. Before the discovery of insulin, it was just a biological fact that diabetics would not live long lives. The obstacles to my barefoot mountaineering are physical facts about the climb and the nature of feet. My parasailing limitations have mainly to do with height and fear. The reason I have felt like an imposter in philosophy and the reason I can't climb Everest barefoot are quite different.

One difference among these barriers is that some of them are internal and some external. The ice on Everest is an external barrier. My fear of heights is an internal barrier. Barriers to value fulfillment also differ in terms of how we evaluate them. Some barriers (such as prejudice) we think are bad and ought not to be there, while others (like the height of a mountain) we are willing to live with. Notice that these "bad barriers" can be internal (sexism may cause me to think I shouldn't be a philosopher) or external (two hundred years ago I would not have been admitted to most universities). Notice also that barriers of any kind vary in terms of how difficult they are to change. Some—the height of Everest, for example—can't be changed at all. Others, like my fear of heights, could be overcome in a few years. Still others, such as prejudice, can be changed over longer periods of time.

Barriers we think should change—and, in particular, unjust or unfair barriers—will be the main focus of this chapter. Living in the sexist culture of today's United States is different in important ways from living in a world in which a person can't climb to the top of Everest in bare feet. Sexist culture is something that many of us value changing, whereas the mountaineering situation is something most of us are very much willing to accept. Unfair social norms are like insects prowling around in your web of values. They need to be strangled in silk, not given a throne to sit on.

To state the obvious, sexism is not the only culprit. There are many different cases in which the fulfillment of values is hindered by something we think is unfair and unnecessary. Think, for instance, about the ways in which racism, a painfully obvious example, affects the values of Black parents in the United States. Recall from chapter 3 Martin Luther King Jr.'s sadness about the ways in which racism harmed his daughter's sense of her own worth. Or think of Black parents having to talk to their sons and daughters about how to behave in order to reduce their risk of being unfairly harassed, or worse, by police. Parents value the welfare of their children and racism impedes this value.

To risk stating the obvious again, injustice is often so deeply entrenched and so limiting that it prevents people from doing anything to change it. For people whose basic needs are not met, injustice may be nearly as unchangeable as the height of a mountain. As I mentioned in the preface to this book, these obstacles are a tremendous impediment to well-being for millions of people in the world, but they are far beyond my expertise. My focus in this chapter is, instead, on how those of us who are fortunate enough to have a choice in the matter should react to the unjust barriers to our own value fulfillment.

It's important to address this topic, because my emphasis on reducing conflict may seem to lead to the wrong advice about it. If sexism is impeding your ability to climb the corporate ladder, stop caring about success in business! If prejudice is making it difficult for you to be taken seriously as a classical musician, give up the violin! After all, if it's good advice for a myopic diabetic to give up wanting to be an astronaut, why wouldn't it also be good advice for women to give up wanting to be philosophers or dentists or corporate executives?

The answer, I think, is that resisting injustice itself is a compelling value: this is not as hopeless as barefoot ice-climbing, it is a goal many of us already care about, and we can find communities of likeminded people who can bolster our sense that it is a worthwhile value to have. Not that it's easy to value fighting for justice: coping with social forces that are bad for us and for others and that we believe could be different introduces new challenges to the process of resolving our value conflicts.

THE REALITY OF SOCIALIZATION, SEXISM, AND CONFLICT

To examine these challenges, let's turn again to the familiar work/life balance problem. This conflict of goals is certainly affected by social expectations and constraints, and it plays out differently for different groups of people. At least in the United States, in the twenty-first century white men have typically been judged for not being ambitious enough. White women, by contrast, have been judged for working too much and not staying home with children, or for choosing not to have children in the first place. Black women are judged for not working enough and for not spending enough quality time with their children, putting them in an impossible double bind. In the workaholic culture of the United States, everyone is judged for spending time on frivolous things that don't make money or for not fulfilling a normal social role. These expectations can limit the possibilities for reinterpreting our values.

Worse, for women, certain values that are encouraged by our culture (caretaking, deference, modesty) are often in stark conflict with career goals (success, remuneration, respect). Many writers and academics have pointed out that female socialization conflicts with career goals; it has been blamed for the wage gap between men and women and for the fact that there are few women in top leadership positions.[1] I would guess that most women reading this book have some personal experience that fits into this category of goal conflict. But I do not think that this example is of interest only to women, because men who value caring for others face similar, though not identical conflicts. (I can't help but notice that my pointing this out is a kind of deference. I have been reading philosophy written mainly by men for thirty years and none of them have ever worried about whether their examples might not work for their female readers!)

In my own case, I have experienced the conflict as one between wanting to be a successful philosopher and wanting to be liked and approved of by others. The moments throughout my career at which these goals have been most obviously opposed stand out in my mind as painful memories. After I argued a point loudly in a graduate school seminar, one of my fellow students, assuming menstruation must explain my reaction, asked me if I was "on the rag." At a dinner at which I expressed my interest in participating in a project for which the colleague sitting beside me had just won a large grant, I was told by a second colleague, "Whoa—down, girl." After a talk I gave at which a psychologist in the audience talked to me at length about a possible collaboration, a colleague of mine commented that the man had likely expressed interest because he wanted to sleep with me. Despite having had experiences like these, I consider myself relatively fortunate. I have never been assaulted or harassed in a way that traumatized me. But the conflict between being a successful philosopher and being socially accepted—a conflict rooted in sexism—was certainly detrimental to my overall value fulfillment.

Happily, some of these experiences diminished with age. Not so happily, new versions of these sexism-fueled conflicts arose as I moved into academic leadership. When women take leadership positions, the conflict plays out against the background of assertive women being perceived as "bossy." I have a pair of pink socks decorated with the message "I'm not bossy. I'm the boss." Why do they make pink socks with this message? I think it's because women who are bosses are called bossy as an insult. Women who tell other people what to do are not upholding the values that women are supposed to cherish; they don't seem nurturing and deferential. When I became chair of my department, I found this conflict difficult to navigate. (Academic department chairs in the liberal arts manage faculty and staff and are responsible for merit reviews, promotions, and the curriculum, among other things; typically, they have a lot of responsibility but very little real power.) I solved the problem by finding a way to make demands that didn't seem threatening, often using self-deprecation and humor to soften the request. This worked, but it was also *exhausting* (and a little demeaning).

I also found myself deeply bothered by the conflicts between my colleagues. These clashes would literally keep me up at night and occupy my every waking second. My desire to get along and to see others getting along, my general aversion to disagreement, made it painful to see intelligent people miscommunicating. What did I do about this? I spent a lot of time and energy thinking about how to help my colleagues get along and steer us all onto the same path. This contributed to my caretaking goals and also to *some* of my career goals (because I think good administrators should manage disagreements in their teams). But it took away from my research and teaching, the two things I have always loved about my job. I had trouble concentrating, couldn't read anything other than email, and wasn't able to think clearly about my own research. Over the past several years, the male colleague who was department chair before me asked me why I wasn't considering extending my service. From his perspective, being chair was very little work and the reduction in teaching duties gave him more time to do his research. I don't think this colleague would disagree that he didn't do the kind of emotional labor that I did. For me, managing relationships took up so much of my time and energy that I had almost none left for writing.

What I have described are intergoal conflicts between being a good philosopher and being a nice person, between career success and caring, between being a good leader and being liked. As such, they are open to the same strategies of adjusting, prioritizing, and reinterpreting that we considered in the previous chapter. But it's important that conflicts such as these are shaped by aspects of the social world that many of us would like to change. This is a crucial difference from the conflicts caused by limited time or aging. Yes, it would be great to have more time, and an extra day in the week would help me resolve some of the conflicts among my values, but there's no injustice here. We all have the same number of hours. Sure, we would all prefer our bodies not to age, but we tend to regard the aging process as natural and inevitable rather than unfair. We try to mitigate the problems it causes us, but we don't tend to identify as "against aging." Unfair social norms in the workplace are not inevitable, however. And many of us do identify as being against prejudice and unfairness.

This is important to how we think about our goals and values in two ways. First, the fact that an unjust social world creates conflict for us is a good reason to adopt a new value: namely, the value of social change. Second, when the social world influencing our goals is an unfair one, it should make us think that our unreflective, culturally encouraged goals—make everyone happy and comfortable! never upset anybody!—are deserving of special scrutiny. If I can see that my desire to please everyone is the result of forces that are not to my benefit, it makes me think that these goals are more in need of change than the ones related to my career.

The first point, about valuing social change, will also be discussed in chapter 8, but it's worth saying a little bit more about it here. Surprisingly, it may help to think again about Millicent. For this to be helpful, we'll have to think of her as a rather sophisticated turtle, a lot more like us than a real one, but still with her simple goals of eating strawberries and being near the stream. Now imagine that the other turtles, having never tasted strawberries and being somewhat closed-minded, don't think too highly of her diet. So, Millicent, in addition to the risk of getting hit by a car, faces the stern disapproval of her peers. This social fact adds another kind of conflict, assuming that Millicent values her community and their approval. How would valuing social change help? First, it highlights that the obstacle is not as fixed as the location of the stream, which makes her interest in strawberries easier to sustain. Second, it reaffirms her belief that there's nothing wrong with her interest in strawberries, at least not in virtue of the social disapproval of her closed-minded, ignorant peers. Third, it reduces the conflict between strawberries and approval. It does this by allowing her to interpret the latter goal as *reasonable approval*, given the flaws of her fellow turtles. It allows her to interpret "eating strawberries" as *making progress toward eating strawberries* in light of the social obstacles she faces.

I do not mean to trivialize oppression by comparing it to the disapproval of turtles. But sometimes a trivial example can help us see something clearly by reducing all the noise created by a real example. In the real world, these same points are true. In my case, valuing ways to change the sexist norms of philosophy has highlighted for me that the conflict I've experienced isn't necessarily permanent. It has affirmed my thought that I'm not crazy for wanting philosophy to be different. It has also reduced the conflict between my desire for approval and my desire to be a good philosopher by leading me to think about being a good philosopher as, in part, a matter of contributing to making philosophy more fair. In general, valuing social change can help people to frame their values in ways that conduce to greater overall fulfillment.

The picture I have been painting may seem to place the burden of social change on the individual experiencing the injustice and suggest that they must value it as a goal. But the reality is that this may not always be possible, and it's certainly not obligatory. Some people are so restricted by unfairness that there is very little they can do. Sometimes unfairness is so entrenched that we can make no progress and *valuing* progress is just demoralizing. To demand that the people who are the most burdened by unjust social arrangements be the ones to fix it is itself very unfair. My point here is simply that if we, as individuals, are able to value social change and to pursue change effectively, it might make things better for us from the point of view of fulfilling our values overall.

It's also worth noting that valuing social change is not only an option for those who are harmed by unfairness. Caring about others in our community often creates conflicts between cultural norms and our values, even if we are not on the receiving end of the unfairness. If Chad's conservative Christian church does not accept his lesbian friend, Chad has a conflict between caring about his friend and belonging to that church. Valuing social change can help him construct a system of values that reduces this conflict by giving him a reason to find a more accepting church or allowing him to see himself as working for change that would help his friend. In general, living in a community that treats some of its members unjustly creates a conflict for anyone who has relationships with people being mistreated or who values living in an ethical community. For people who are relatively privileged, this conflict may not be as easy to see as one between, say, going to the office and staying home with a sick child, but it's there. It may cause unacknowledged feelings of guilt or shame, or just sadness and disappointment. Prioritizing social change in your system of values can help to make sense of these feelings and to see them as an appropriate response to injustice rather than as a sign that you're living your life wrong.

FIGURING OUT WHAT MATTERS
IN AN UNFAIR CULTURE

Recognizing when unfair cultural norms have shaped our values has a second upshot: the need for special scrutiny of those values and the internal barriers they impose. What does this look like? How, for example, should women think about the values of caring, kindness, and modesty?

Before we tackle this question, let me take a moment to acknowledge that not everyone is shaped by culture in the same way—I certainly know women who have not internalized harmful versions of these values to the degree that I have. The influence of culture interacts with people's unique experiences and their individual personalities. In my case, growing up with a chronic illness had a profound influence. The technology to manage diabetes when I was a kid was not nearly as good as it is now, and it was easy to see myself as fragile. Worse, the specialists I saw when I was a small child communicated to me that if I didn't conform exactly to their expectations—*if I didn't make them happy*, was how I saw it at age five—I would go blind and lose my toes. These features of my early life encouraged deep internalization of norms of deference and pleasing other people. Some women get that encouragement from their parents, their church, their school, while others are strongly encouraged to resist. Similarly, men's personalities and individual experiences will influence how much they internalize norms of self-sufficiency and toughness; indeed, I know some men who relate more to my experience than they do to John Wayne. These differences are important, but at the same time there are common patterns worth discussing.

Acknowledging the context prompts some questions: How do I interpret these values? Who benefits from the way that I understand the requirements of caring, kindness, and modesty? Are these values interpreted the same way by everyone? I have tended (not consciously) to interpret caring and kindness as demanding that I never upset or disappoint anyone, and modesty as requiring that I never promote my own professional interests. A person who tries never to upset anyone, and who never puts her own interests first, may be a nice person to work with. However, the goal of never disappointing anyone is just not compatible with career success on any understanding of what that is, nor is it compatible with mental health. The same is true for the goal of being liked by everyone and the goal of avoiding upsetting people or making them angry. Unless the only thing you value is not upsetting other people, these are dysfunctional ways of interpreting the values of caring, kindness, and modesty. There is so much you cannot do if you're not willing to risk upsetting anyone. As the bumper sticker says, "Well behaved women seldom make history."[2]

At the same time, caring, kindness, and modesty are not to be discarded like ugly weeds. I don't want to be an arrogant jerk, even if it would eliminate the conflict with my career goals! Reinterpretation of caring, kindness, and modesty seems like the right strategy here. If sexism has shaped what I think these values require, perhaps I could learn to rethink them as requiring something that isn't in conflict with being a good philosopher or a good leader or with mental health. And surely this is possible. The heart of kindness is consideration of other people's needs and interests. This does not have to mean always putting their interests first, or catering to their every whim. The key to modesty is not thinking that you are better than everyone else and that what you have to say is more important. This does not require thinking that you are less worthy than anyone else. The general values encouraged by unfair socialization do not have to be understood as imposing unfair requirements.

Notice that in the conflict between stereotypically feminine values and career goals, the notions of career success may have to shift, too. The meaning of "a good philosopher" or "an effective leader" is also shaped by cultural norms that are unfair to women (and also to men of color, though in different ways). But there are other ways of interpreting success. This is particularly clear when it comes to managing other people. Good bosses care about helping their employees do their best work. Good managers lead by motivating their colleagues as part of a team, rather than by imposing their authority. Imagining an effective leader who is also caring, kind, and modest isn't so strange. A kind, caring, and modest philosopher may be a bit more of a stretch, but we have made some progress since I was a graduate student!

Men experience comparable sorts of conflict that prompt special scrutiny. They tend to be socialized to value independence, strength, and confidence, and to interpret these values in particular ways. For my father's generation, strength was exemplified by John Wayne and it included not just physical strength but also a kind of mental toughness that was incompatible with showing any emotions. This kind of socialization may be less intense than it was in my father's day, but it hasn't disappeared. Listen to Robert Vaughn, a nurse who was interviewed by Shankar Vedantam in 2020 on an episode of the podcast *Hidden Brain*.[3] Vaughn observes:

> I think a lot of guys who might go into health care are interested in health and fitness. They're interested in being healthy, being fit, being active. And so they're doing a lot of—they're running marathons. They're doing weightlifting competitions. They're doing bodybuilding competitions. And I think part of it may also be showing, hey, you know, I'm not this—I'm not sure of the wording I want to use for it. I'm not a guy who is this meek or—I don't know—I'm not effeminate, or I'm not this nurse stereotype. Maybe it's pushing against the stereotype of what you might assume a male nurse would be. And so it's saying, you know what? I'm not that. I'm actually pretty manly in other aspects.

Vaughn is suggesting that for some men who work as caregivers, appearing stereotypically masculine is a goal. Psychologist Jennifer Bosson, interviewed in the same podcast, has found that it's often a hidden motivation. Bosson, who researches masculinity, did an experiment in which she had one group of men do a stereotypically feminine activity (braiding hair), while the other group did a more "manly" activity (braiding rope).[4] The men in both groups were told that they were being videotaped and that these tapes would be watched by others later for research purposes. Once the braiding task was complete, the men were told they would do another activity, but they could choose between a brainteaser game and hitting a punching bag. According to Bosson, men who braided hair were much more likely to choose punching afterward than men who braided rope. Her explanation for these findings is that avoiding being perceived as weak or feminine was operating as a nonconscious goal, which was activated in the men who did something (braiding hair) that threatened it.

If Bosson is right, some male nurses experience a conflict between their professional goals and a hidden goal of adhering to stereotypes of masculinity. One thing such a nurse could do would be to stop nursing and become a truck driver, or a construction worker, or a dentist. But this doesn't seem like the best solution to the conflict just described, particularly for someone who has invested years in training and who finds the work really rewarding. Alternatively, in the male nurse's case, and in my own, it may be possible to change the hidden motivations or parts of our personality that make life difficult for us. Recognizing that his underlying aspiration to be like John Wayne is the product of an unfair culture, a man in a caregiving profession could attempt to rid himself of that aspiration.

Purging goals can be difficult, though, as we know. So, once again, we can consider the strategy of reinterpreting the values that are in conflict. Taking up stereotypically masculine hobbies may be one sensible way to do this if it means that "masculinity" is understood as having to do with fitness rather than work. This reinterpretation will be effective if it achieves the underlying goal of being "manly" without sacrificing the value of work (or other important values such as relationships with other people). This can be a good way to reduce conflict, particularly if the "manly" hobbies are enjoyable and suited to the person. There are certainly more destructive ways of proving one's masculinity. Identifying the conflicting goals and recognizing that lifting weights, for example, is a way of attaining one goal without sacrificing another is an achievement of self-understanding that may even discourage destructive habits. If a man knows *why* he's lifting weights, he will be better prepared to deal with an injury or other setback that takes this hobby away from him. Someone who can't change his conception of masculinity may be better off replacing weightlifting with something else that makes him feel good about himself.

Male socialization causes other conflicts, too. Men who are taught to think they have to be independent, strong, and confident may have hidden goals of never asking for help or admitting they don't know something. These goals can conflict with all sorts of values, including being an emotionally attuned parent.[5] The process of reinterpreting values works here too. Are there weeds than can be identified and pulled? If not, are there values that can be reinterpreted to reduce conflict? Can asking for help be seen as a kind of strength, because it requires defying others' expectations? Can admitting you don't know something be seen as part of confidence because you are secure enough to admit to your weaknesses? Once again, paying attention to the way that the social world influences our values recommends that we give special scrutiny to those values and to ask questions we might not otherwise have asked.

———

Our communities and cultures shape our values in unavoidable ways. Sometimes this creates conflicts that make it difficult for us to fulfill our values. Understanding our social reality can help us see the value in opposing unjust barriers, even if they are not easy to change. It can also help us by providing some self-understanding. Recognizing these forces for what they are can help us see opportunities that might not be noticeable if we thought of them as neutral, natural obstacles such as the height of a mountain. Of course, the forces of culture that make us who we are may be undesirable and less permanent than a mountain, but they are still powerful. We might wonder what happens when our strategies of identification, refinement, and reinterpretation don't work. We'll consider some options in chapter 6.

6

WHEN ALL ELSE FAILS

Let's take stock. It's good for us to be able to do the things that matter to us. We're not always clear about what matters, or what matters most, or how it matters, and the experience of conflict pushes us to find clarity. We refine our system of values and goals by seeing clearly what they are, adjusting how we go about achieving them, getting rid of the bad stuff, and reinterpreting what our values mean so that we can pursue them together. What do we do when these strategies fail? What can we do about perpetual conflicts that we can't reduce using any of these methods? Do these failures mean we aren't on the right path?

MAKING PEACE WITH WHAT YOU CAN'T CHANGE

Some readers, in response to my confessions about the experience of academic leadership, may have thought that I should stop being so damned sensitive! Stop caring what other people think! If I could have let go of some of the goals that female (and diabetic) socialization encouraged in me, I could have taken the money and run! (At many universities, including mine, you get extra pay to be the department chair.) Certainly there are women who have resisted the internalization of feminine norms more successfully than I have.

But, in the words of Popeye the Sailor Man, I am what I am, and what I am is stuck with some internal conflicts. In general, we can't do things that we can't do, and our goals and hidden motives can be remarkably tenacious. That being the case, what do we do if we think we ought to stop caring so much about what everyone else thinks, or about making a lot of money, but we just can't make much progress?

A second-best strategy for dealing with goals that we identify as undesirable but unmovable is to try to see the humor in our imperfection. For example, let's say you're a male nurse who comes to realize that your interest in weight-lifting is due in part to a desire to appear masculine. And let's imagine that you don't really like this about yourself—you don't see traditional masculinity as an important value that you should uphold—but you also realize that it's a pretty sticky part of your personality. One option is to embrace this aspect of yourself without really endorsing it, as you might do with a friend's flaws. We do this with friends all the time: "Oh, that's just Dom. They're anxious about money and it makes them annoying when you're paying a restaurant bill, but they're not actually a stingy person." "Yeah, Walter is weirdly snobby about wine, but you can tease him about it." Similarly, we can acknowledge the aspects of ourselves that are in tension with what really matters to us, tease ourselves about them, and try not to let them motivate us to do anything that's harmful. You can smile at yourself for wanting to be manly while enjoying your strength and the admiring stares you get at the gym.

Humor should be accompanied by a little compassion. I can sympathize with the puny little me who wants everyone to like her and who feels as though she's not good enough to be where she is. Welcome to the party, imposter syndrome![1] This comes from a guided meditation I once listened to. The meditation expert, Jeff Warren, suggested to his listeners that when we identify a bad feeling or thought, we "welcome it to the party" of thoughts and feelings, without judgment. This is similar to laughing at the parts of ourselves that we wish we didn't have; it's a way of decreasing their power by taking away their central role as our enemy. If the meditation experts are correct, welcoming these undesirable parts of ourselves to "the party"— accepting who we are without being too self-critical, having a sense of humor about it—may also be a good way to loosen the hold of our undesirable features. I do find that once I name what I'm feeling "imposter syndrome," the feelings of inferiority diminish.

In effect, what we're doing when we "make peace" with some aspect of ourselves in these ways is demoting it. We're saying, "This desire to please everyone is not a value, it's a quirk of my personality" or "this concern for traditional masculinity is not a priority, it's the result of harmful socialization." This is why making peace doesn't cause us to be unsettled about our values, even though it doesn't resolve the conflict completely. Generally, as we've seen, conflict gives rise to doubt about our values; it spurs us to investigate and refine what matters to us. When we agree to live with some part of ourselves that is in conflict with important goals, the conflict is still there, but the bite is taken out of it.

Making peace doesn't mean just living with goals you reject and letting them take up a lot of space in your life. The "make peace with it" strategy is not the easy way out. Making peace means refusing to commit to your undesirable goal as a value.

This requires some effort. It's easy to get swept back into old patterns in which that sticky, unhelpful part of yourself is running the show. Inviting my inner pleaser to the party is not the same thing as inviting her to the leadership circle, and I have to be on guard against her trying to take over. As we saw in the last chapter, we can help ourselves out here by explicitly valuing changing the ugly forces that created the patterns we don't like. I find it easier to keep my inner pleaser in the demotion zone when I am working against the norms that create more inner pleasers.

Think about gardening again. Some of the features of our personalities are a bit like the weather—there's just not much you can do about them. You can't grow rhubarb in the desert, and I can't be straightforwardly assertive without feeling a little bit bad about myself. More generally, for most of us there are things we value that we wish we didn't have to care about, or that we wish we could value differently, that nevertheless limit how it's possible for us to reshape our other goals. The path forward to value fulfillment is to make compromises you can live with given where you are.

But is this the only path?

RADICAL CHANGE

One thing we can say about the strategies we've considered so far is that they are conservative. Whether we are identifying bad values, reinterpreting good values, or looking for confirmation that we have the right values, we are always relying on other values we have. I've said this a few times. There's no value-free perspective we can take to assess all of our values at once. But what if our values are wrong *all the way down*?

What if what we really need is a complete overhaul, or at least a big change to something very basic and central to our system of values? What if our values were planted in a toxic waste site and we need to uproot the old oak trees and replace all the soil?

It's not impossible that the life in which a person can get the most value fulfillment is one in which that person undergoes a radical change of values: a "value system transplant," we might say. People whose values have been shaped by external forces that are insensitive to their interests may end up with values so unsuitable that they can't get to a better set just by tinkering with the ones they have. Unfortunately, many people who are in this situation will not have the freedom to experiment. If your values have been successfully shaped by an abusive family or an oppressive culture, your freedom to imagine alternatives may also be curtailed. This is a serious moral problem that really requires a book of its own (and, indeed, many books have been written about it).[2] Our focus in the remainder of this chapter will be on people who are able to consider dramatic changes.

I have not experienced a radical change in my own values, so I don't have any personal experience to draw on here. Instead, my thoughts on this subject have been influenced by memoirs and stories about people whose values have been fundamentally challenged. One particularly illuminating case comes from Tara Westover's wonderful memoir, *Educated*.[3] Westover was raised by fundamentalist Mormon parents who had delusions of impending Armageddon and did not believe in Western medicine. The father of the family was a scrap metal collector who put his children at tremendous risk carting dangerous heavy objects. Many of them had accidents, were seriously injured, and then received no effective treatment. The values Westover inherited from her parents literally made her sick, injured her body, and prevented her from getting an education, which was something she craved.

Reading this memoir, there were many points at which it was hard for me to understand why she found it so difficult to run as far away as she could from her crazy and dangerous family. But her book also illustrates how incredibly challenging radical change can be, even if it seems like the obvious choice from the outside. In the end, Westover had to cut ties with many members of her family. Still, there was genuine love involved, and this often caused her to doubt her rebellious plans. She grew up valuing her family and her relationships with her parents and siblings. That means she grew up caring about them and thinking that they mattered to the quality of her own life. Values, even those that need to be changed, are held in place by an integrated pattern of emotions, desires, and judgments. A radical change will shake the earth, and it's very hard to choose to do something that disturbs the ground you walk on.

Westover's experience is extreme, but in broad outline, it is one shared by anyone who breaks with her family, religion, or culture for the sake of other values. LGBTQ people whose families reject them are often in this position. They make new lives and reject many of the friendships, communities, ideals of character, and other values with which they grew up. Revolutionaries and activists who rebel against their culture have to make a radical change in the values that they share with the culture in which they were raised. Divorce is sometimes the result of a radical change in values, especially for women who pursue it because they come to see how their marriage is shaped by sexist norms. A woman who realizes that she does all the housework, that her needs always come second, and that her husband is not actually very interested in what she wants may decide that the only self-respecting path forward is to end the marriage. This is not a simple shift in values, especially if there are children in the family—swap out a husband for a paid handyman and a few boyfriends and voilà! At least for some women, divorce can be a radical change because it impinges on so many things, from self-image to financial security to vacation plans.

As these examples suggest, "radical" value change is a matter of degree. But what they have in common is that something central to the person's web of values is no good and needs to be changed. Until this point, we have relied on ultimate values as touchstones in the process of refining our systems of goals. Now the question is what to do if we can't rely on those touchstones. What if some of our ultimate values (family, marriage, faith, community) are precisely the ones that are making us miserable? What do we do then?

Someone whose basic values are hurting them is like someone who is being tossed by a powerful wave—they need something to hang onto, to tell them which direction is up. If you've never been tossed by a wave, I can tell you that it's an incredibly disorienting experience! I think something similar must happen to people who have reason to doubt their basic values. So, the question of what to do is really a question of what to hold on to. What can we trust?

We might hope that someone will throw us a rope. But there are two problems with ropes: someone has to be holding the other end, and you have to decide to grab hold. If you're drowning and desperate, you'll grab onto anything, but that doesn't settle the question of what's good for you. I think that the question of what to hang on to has to be settled by something we're already holding. Now that I've stretched this metaphor as far is it will go, let me make the point directly: when our basic values are harmful to us, we can change them by appealing to even more basic features of our goal-seeking nature. We can understand radical shifts in values as responding to very basic goals that we can't psychologically do without.

The psychology of our goal-seeking nature, as discussed in chapter 2, will come in handy to explain this. There are some basic psychological motivations that almost every one of us has and has had since we were a baby. These are our needs for comfort and security, novelty and excitement, autonomy (control over our life), competence (the skills to do what we want to do), and affiliation with other people. These are things we can hang on to when we are at sea.

Our feelings are another basic building block. Recall that what it is to value something includes the tendency to have good feelings about it. Part of what it is to value family is to feel happy about spending time with them. Part of what it is to value your work is to feel proud of it when you do a good job. To value running is to enjoy it. To value being a parent is to feel pride when your kid tells you you're the best mom or dad. To value music is to be excited when you have the opportunity to see your favorite band play live. Feelings are an essential part of our capacity to value anything. That means that if we are looking to make a radical change, we are going to have to find something we will respond to emotionally.

So, if we are questioning some fairly central goals and values, we still have something to anchor us: our basic motivations and our feelings. In one way of looking at it, these basic motivations and feelings are a bedrock foundation, something we can rely on unconditionally in order to build up a better system of values. As you might guess at this point in the book, I'm not a great believer in bedrock foundations when it comes to values. Nevertheless, I do think these basic motivations and our feelings provide a kind of raft we can rely on if we are considering a radical change. The idea is that these things are the most stable platform we have and relying on them is better than drowning.

It strikes me that this makes sense of the experiences that Tara Westover reports. What did she hang on to while she was in such a turbulent phase of her life? How did she do this? She relied on her own motivations and feelings—the physical pain caused by her father and brother, the love of her other siblings who were suffering because of their father, and her tremendous curiosity about the world. Her intellectual curiosity led her to figure out how to get admitted to Brigham Young University without a high school diploma and, ultimately, to earn a PhD in history at Cambridge University in England. *Educated* is the title of her book and it's also one of the goals (initially hidden to her) that allowed her to change many of her values.

People raised in hostile communities that do not support them can also rely on basic needs and feelings as anchors. Many LGBTQ people maintain the value of "family" by reinterpreting this to mean "chosen family." Basic affiliative goals anchor a shift to a new set of people who allow the person to fulfill their other goals and to feel supported in doing so. Women who get a divorce because they come to see their marriages as oppressive hang on to the values of self-respect, autonomy, and their own competence. These shifts have significant costs: giving up something that has been a basic value is a real loss, even if the promise is that you will have greater fulfillment in the future with your significantly revised set of values. But there are costs on both sides and changing a basic value may still be better than the alternative.

———

To review, to live our lives well we need to be able to pursue and achieve the things that really matter to us. In other words, we need to be able to fulfill our goals, and especially our most important goals—our values. Once we can identify our values and what the conflicts are, we have a strategy for solving our problem. We examine our minor goals, beliefs, and desires for their relationship to our core values, identify and eliminate goals and values that are not consistent with our core values, and make use of the enormous flexibility of our brains to re-interpret our values so that they harmonize with our beliefs, feelings, and circumstances. When we can't achieve harmony with what we have, we can consider strategies for making peace or making radical change. But even when radical change is the best option, we have to work with who we are.

7

THE VALUE OF OTHERS

If you've stuck with me so far, which I guess you have, you'll probably have noticed that I haven't told you what you ought to value. I haven't wanted to assume that there are facts about values "out there" that we are trying to discover as we might discover the natural diet of turtles. I haven't wanted to assume it, because I don't believe it; I think that it's we valuers who determine what matters. This may make you think "anything goes!" In particular, it may make you think that human beings do well thinking about themselves and pursuing their goals without a thought to other people. Perhaps the idea that what matters depends on the person to whom it matters suggests a kind of rugged individualism.

But "anything goes!" is absolutely not the right conclusion to draw. We've already seen that, because we are human beings who have developed in the ways that human beings do, the vast majority of us will have values that include comfort and security, novelty and excitement, autonomy, competence, and affiliation with other people. We can find new ways to pursue these values, but we can't just slough them off like dead skin. They are part of who we are. Affiliation has been in the background of most of my examples, but we haven't yet focused on it specifically. For just about everybody, the need for relationships is crucial.

The need for affiliation with other people also has special significance. This is because our dependence on other people not only has implications for how our own lives go, but also for how we treat other people. In this chapter, we'll talk about the different ways in which other people are intertwined with our values, and what this means for how we should treat others.

OTHER PEOPLE IN OUR GARDENS

We all know that human beings are social creatures. We are born weak and puny, and we stay relatively weak (compared to the threats against us) throughout our lives. We wouldn't have survived as a species if we didn't work in groups, so we have evolved many "groupish" tendencies. Evolutionary biologist Joseph Henrich argues that the reason the human species has been so successful in terms of evolution is our social intelligence.[1] Without our ability to cooperate and learn from each other, he writes, we would not have spread to every ecological niche on the planet. For individual people, the fact that we are a "social species" means that we care a lot about other people and what they think of us. By and large, we want to belong. We want to hang out with our fellow humans. We want other people to like us.

There has been quite a bit of social scientific research on our need for affiliation. Every psychological or philosophical theory of well-being that provides a list of goods includes affiliation, friendships, or relationships as one of the basic human goods.[2] We care about each other, we do things together, and we learn from each other. Other people are in our gardens.

Now, of course, sometimes they are in our gardens trampling on our plants. Other people can be obstacles to our value fulfillment. This is not difficult to see, and we've already seen a number of examples of it in the last two chapters. Sexist norms, reinforced by other people, constrain what women and girls are able to achieve. Other people's racism curtails what Black people can achieve and threatens their very lives. Some closed-minded and inflexible parents prevent their children from being who they really are. And there are plenty of mundane examples: my husband's lack of interest in dessert put the kibosh on my goal of making fancy cakes for someone other than myself, my Zumba teacher's schedule means I can't enjoy her choreography any time I want, my sister's moving to L.A. prevents me from seeing her as often as I would like. But part of the reason other people can block us is precisely that they are so enmeshed in what we care about. I don't want to eat cake by myself, or dance alone, or see my sister once a year. However much other people are impediments to fulfilling our goals, we couldn't live without them.

For most of us, then, other people are in our systems of values in at least two different ways. First, we value other people for themselves. Second, we value activities that depend on the participation and the approval of other people. On the first point, if you're a parent, it will be obvious to you that you value other people for their own sakes. I remember my father telling me that if he could have been diabetic instead of me, he would have done so without a second thought. I'm pretty sure he was telling the truth about this and not just saying it because he knew it was impossible anyway. People make tremendous sacrifices for their children because they care about their children's well-being. Of course, it's true that we evolved to feel this way about our children—parents who weren't willing to sacrifice anything for their offspring didn't succeed in passing on their genes. But that's not relevant to the values we have now. My dad cares about me and wants me to do well because he loves me—that's his *reason*—not because he is the product of evolution. Evolution might be what has caused people to have these tendencies to care about their children so much, but it isn't part of our own narrative of why we value the people we value.

I don't have children, but I do care about other people for their own sakes. I care about the lives of my parents, my husband, my sisters, my nieces and nephews, my friends, and even some of my academic colleagues! I don't just care about them because they make me happy (they don't always). I do, of course, get something out of these relationships—my sisters make me laugh, my friend Lisa never forgets my birthday, and so on—but that doesn't totally capture the way that I value them. I want them to do well, and I feel happy when they flourish *because* they are flourishing. I find that some of my first-year ethics students get hung up here about the fact that if I want these people to be happy, then their happiness is just something I want for selfish reasons (because I want it!). But this is a basic philosophical mistake: the fact that I desire something doesn't mean that what I desire is my own benefit. Sometimes, the object of my desire—the goal that is represented as good—is someone else's happiness or success. I may be happy when I get it, but that doesn't change the fact that what I want in the first place is for the other person to be happy or successful.[3] So, we value other people directly. I'm not saying that everyone necessarily values other people in this way, but most of us do.

The second way that other people get into our value systems has to do with the ways that many of our other values depend on other people. This is because so many of the things we value have a social dimension. This is pretty obvious when it comes to group activities. If you value any kind of team sports, you have to find other people to play with. If you value being in a choir, band, or orchestra, you are dependent on other musicians. If you value your membership in a religious community, you are counting on other people to worship along with you. And so on for so many human activities.

We can see our mutual dependence even in the valued activities that we do entirely alone. I value writing, which is a very solitary activity. Indeed, I can't work within earshot of my husband (an issue during the COVID-19 lockdown) because he's very fidgety and his fidgeting makes noise. But most people who write anticipate an audience. Writing is primarily about communicating something to other people, and so their opinions at some point matter to one's success as a writer. One of my colleagues is a Lego enthusiast. He builds amazing models and mosaics out of Lego blocks. This is a solitary activity, but my colleague builds for others, enters Lego competitions, and writes about Lego on blogs. Running can be a very solitary sport, but the runners I know join running groups and download apps that connect them to other runners so they can talk about their runs. Avid weightlifters go to gyms where they can compare results, dancers take dance classes, cooks cook for other people and read cooking blogs. Even people who love to read novels (a solitary activity if ever there was one) join book clubs!

We also value ways of being in the world—aspects of our own character—that depend on other people. Most people want not just to *have* friends but also to *be* a good friend. You aren't a good friend if your friends think you're an untrustworthy egomaniac. Now, it's certainly possible to have a relationship with another person in which it makes no difference what the other person thinks of you as a friend. But would this really be a friendship? Even if it would, it's not the kind of friendship I would want. You might have friends who care about you for your money, your good looks, or your connections, who don't care how good a friend you are. But if you want friends who care about you for your own sake in the long term, you have to care about them too. It's the same with families (whether biological or chosen) and relationships with family members—parents want to be successful parents, sons and daughters want to be loving sons and daughters, team members want to be team players, and so on. The way we value many of our relationships is multidimensional. We care about the people themselves, we care about what we do together, and we care about the way we are in relation to them. Many of the things we care about depend on the responses of other people.

So, many of our values depend on other people in all sorts of ways. What other people do and say and think about us makes a difference as to whether we can fulfill many of our values. We need the people we love to be healthy and there for us. We need other people to be in our lives, participating in activities with us. We need the approval of (some) others. This is not a flaw or a weakness to be overcome. It's just what we are like.

What is more, it's a part of us that we tend to *like*. Unlike our desire for high-fat foods and salt, our evolved affiliative nature is something that almost all of us embrace if we reflect on the matter. To see this, consider what it would be like to reject our groupish tendencies and reliance on other people. Picture someone who has no values that include other people. Someone who cares only about power, or money, or succeeding at something at any cost to others. It's difficult to find people like this in real life (though there are some recent well-known examples), but fictional characters in this vein—think of Ebenezer Scrooge—tend to be judged harshly before they are taught a lesson. It's not a kind of life that anyone with the values that we all have could aspire to or admire.

Or, consider someone who shares all of your values and is not in any way bothered when other people think she's on the wrong track. All of this person's friends believe she belongs to the wrong church, her entire family thinks her being a baseball fan is a waste of time, her spouse thinks her goals for financial security are completely unrealistic, and everyone she knows thinks she supports the wrong political causes. Also, no one thinks she is a very good friend, daughter, wife, or sister. What's more, this person doesn't care what they think. She does not believe that other people's opinions matter to her values. Can we even imagine such a person? A person who cares about "friendship" but not about her friends' opinions? A person who cares about political causes, but isn't interested in what her community thinks about them? A person who values her faith, but doesn't care that she has no one to share it with? It is difficult to imagine, but even if we can, my point here is that it doesn't seem like an attractive way to live.

To sum up, we humans are social creatures whose well-being is very much dependent on other people. What does this mean for our questions about what to value and how to resolve conflicts among our goals? It means that not all options are equally good. Those that respect our need for affiliation are more likely to succeed. And this means that it can be helpful to consider our need for affiliation, and the other people in our lives, when we reflect on or interpret our values. This is not to say that we should forget about our own interests, talents, likes, and dislikes—these things are also important—but other people are a bigger part of our value systems than we might have thought and this matters for our conflict resolving strategy.

It matters in some obvious ways. Lots of self-help advice suggests that if we want to change something about our lives—to quit smoking, exercise more, learn to knit—we should find other people with whom to share these goals. If you can work out with a friend, or while your children are playing soccer, or as part of a club, you're more likely to enjoy it and to keep doing it. Less obviously, if we want to reject the values of our community (an oppressive family or an unaccepting religious community) because they are frustrating our values, we would do well to find a new community to support us.

We've been talking about how the other people in our gardens influence the kind of gardening we should do. I want to turn now to what we should do for other people's gardens.

OTHER PEOPLE'S VALUES

I've been operating on the assumption that I'm talking to people who do care about other people. If you do, does my approach to value and goal conflict give us any guidance about how we should treat them? Does the value approach that I have presented tell us anything about whether we should help other people tend their gardens, or how to go about it? The first question has a quick answer: If you think that fulfilling values is important to a person's life going well, you should want to help the people you care about fulfill their values too. That's just what it is to want what's best for those people. *How* to do that is more complicated.

Let's consider the easy case first, one in which you think the values of your friend or loved one are pretty decent. Your friend values the same sorts of things you do, though in tolerably different ways, and you think she's on a good path, value-wise. One way to help is by doing things that materially improve your friend's ability to fulfill the clearly identified and valued goals that she has. It's easy to do this when you are part of the values yourself. If your friend values *you* and your friendship, you can help her fulfill that value just by being her friend and doing the kinds of things friends do. But even if you're not part of it, there are things you can do. You can help your friends who are parents by babysitting their kids. You can help your friend achieve her dream of climbing Mount Everest by contributing to her GoFundMe campaign. You can tell your knitting friend about a new yarn store, ask your running friend about his marathon training, eat your baking friend's latest loaf of bread. You can help friends do all sorts of things just by being encouraging and supportive.

The approach outlined in this book introduces a second way to help. We can help our friends achieve their values by talking through their conflicts with them and helping them figure out what's at stake and what their options are for resolving them. In other words, we can help them by engaging with them in the strategy for resolving conflicts. In chapter 3, we talked about how we can learn from other people what values suit us best, because other people sometimes see things about us that we miss. Of course, they can also learn from us. We can share our observations about what our friends seem to be energized by and what seems to lay them low.

Recall that a crucial part of the strategy for resolving conflicts is reinterpreting our values so that they fit better together. We can help friends here, too. We can help them see options for how to reinterpret their values that they may not have considered. Perhaps the friend who wants to climb Everest hasn't considered other, closer, equally interesting mountains. Perhaps your running friend just tore his ACL and you can introduce him to sports that are easier on the knees. Perhaps your friend who is running herself ragged trying to be a perfect mom could stand to hear more about your keep-'em-fed-and-clothed style of parenting. We can help friends reframe their choices as changes rather than admissions of failure. Friends can help each other see success differently, and the mutual approval helps to make this reframing seem resilient rather than pathetic.

WHEN OTHER PEOPLE DON'T MAKE SENSE: A PLEA FOR HUMILITY

It isn't too difficult to figure out how to help loved ones whose values are simpatico. The trickier case is what to do when the people we care about have values we don't really understand or approve of.

Perhaps because of my philosophical interests, I enjoy reading about people I can't understand. A few years ago, I learned that no one had ever crossed Antarctica alone, without help from other people or engines. To me, this is very unsurprising and uninteresting. I'm sure there are many things no one has ever done that I would not want to do in a million years. But to Colin O'Brady (a 33-year-old American adventure athlete) and Louis Rudd (a 49-year-old British Army captain) the fact that no one had ever crossed Antarctica unsupported was *very* interesting. Indeed, this fact motivated them both to try to do it! When I first became aware of their stories, both men were in the midst of attempting this 921-mile journey, pulling their sleds of supplies on cross-country skis across an icy, unforgiving terrain. Happily, they both succeeded. O'Brady completed the trip in fifty-four days, Rudd in fifty-six. That's almost two months of vigorous workout in a freezer under the constant threat of death. Even in light of their survival and record-setting, nothing about this sounds remotely appealing to me.

O'Brady and Rudd both have wives; Rudd has children. They probably also have friends. If they were *my* friends, I would have tried to talk them out of attempting what seems to me a crazy thing to do. If Rudd were my friend, I would even want to prevent him from going. I would consider lying to him if that would change his course: "Louis, you can't go to Antarctica this year because you'll miss my wedding/Broadway debut/bat mitzvah!" I wouldn't want my friend to risk his life in this way, but what about what he wants?

One thing seems clear from the stories you read about people like O'Brady and Rudd—or Alex Honnold (star of the movie *Free Solo*) who climbed the El Capitán monolith without ropes or safety gear. It's really important to them to do these things. So important that many of them keep climbing, trekking, and risking their lives even after someone they know dies in the attempt. (In fact, Louis Rudd's friend Henry Worsley did die attempting the Antarctic crossing in 2016, two years before Rudd set off with the same goal.) These men value risk, adventure, and challenge in the way that I value safety and spending time with my friends and family. I really don't understand them.

We can probably all think of people we love whose values and goals we question: friends who are pursuing careers they seem to hate, offspring at college who are majoring in subjects we don't see the value of, spouses who are spending way too much pursuing some leisure activity we think is a waste of time, and so on. There are certainly times when our friends are on the wrong path and we could help set them on a better one. This is sometimes a good thing to do, and we'll return to this point in a bit. But first, I want to make a plea for humility. A plea for having an open mind about what other people value and for not thinking we know everything about what's good for them. I think that if I were actually Louis Rudd's or Colin O'Brady's friend, as difficult as it would be for me to do, I ought to have some humility about what I think should matter to them.

One reason not to tell people what they should value and how they should live their lives is that it's pushy, rude, and unwelcome. Even if we're *right* about what would be best for others, this is not a great strategy. And, of course, we're often not right, which is another reason to have some humility. There's just a ton of stuff to know and we actually don't know everything. Especially relevant is the fact that we don't know what it's like to be someone else. Apparently, Alex Honnold's brain doesn't react to danger in the same way that typical brains do. It takes a lot to make him feel fear. As someone who is afraid to climb a tree, I have absolutely no idea what that would be like. Parents whose children defy them by majoring in history or philosophy instead of pre-med prob-ably don't know what it's like to be utterly bored by biology classes. I'm sure the women who have told me that I made a mistake not having children have no idea what it's like to live life in the absence of powerful maternal instincts. Given that the best values for a person are the ones that suit that per-son's emotions, desires, and thoughts, and given that we don't always know these things about other people, we can be quite ignorant about what values are best for others.

A nice thing about cultivating humility is that just *trying* to do it puts you on the path to having the virtue. As soon as you think to yourself that you should try to be more cautious about how much you understand other people's goals, you have al-ready admitted that you don't know everything. With humil-ity, trying is a large part of the battle.

It's difficult to accurately assess one's own humility or lack thereof. I do know that I have been called bossy by my younger sisters, and I have to admit, with some shame, that I do have some judgmental tendencies. But thinking about human goal-seeking behavior and humility professionally has made me think I ought to try to curb whatever judgy "know-it-all" tendencies I have. I have tried by adopting some strategic intentions in conversation with other people. Ask questions. Don't give advice if I'm not asked for it, but if I can't resist, pause and think first. Think about how I'd want someone to respond to me if I were the one sharing some problem or concern.

According to one of the few psychological studies on cul-tivating humility, another good strategy might be to reflect on your own limitations and your place in the grand scheme of things.[4] This advice is familiar from certain religious traditions where humility is prized. To be clear, the kind of humility we need to be good friends is not self-abnegation or meekness. But thinking about how limited we are in what we know about the world could be helpful in encouraging us to approach other people with less arrogance.

Are there times when we shouldn't be so open-minded about other people's values? Are there times we *should* tell our loved ones how to live their lives? Yes. Or, at least, there are times we should try to get them to change how they are living their lives in whatever way will be effective (which may not be *telling* them anything). When it makes sense to protest someone else's values or even to intervene in their life is a tricky question that does not admit of a simple answer. But we can identify some guideposts.

We all know of cases in which a person's goals are self-destructive or (as I would put it in goal-seeking terms) antithetical to their overall success in pursuing their values. People who are addicted to harmful substances, partnered with abusive spouses, or thoughtlessly engage in high-risk activities for trivial gain are pursuing short-term goals that will hinder their long-term value fulfillment. (Notice that what counts as "trivial" is a judgment call; Alex Honnold does not see the benefit of free climbing as trivial, for example.) Generally, the more the person's goal is truly hindering her in the long term, and the more certain you are about that, the more you are warranted in taking some kind of stand against that goal. Literal, coercive intervention (of the sort loved ones perform for an alcoholic friend or family member) is a last resort and it's not the only option. We can tell the person what we think, we can withdraw support, or we can offer alternatives to replace the bad goal.

Another type of case is one in which the goals our friend is pursuing are so contradictory to our own most basic values that we cannot sit by and watch them do it. One example of this is immoral goals. Given how most of us feel about killing innocent people, we cannot be open-minded and humble about a friend's interest in becoming an assassin. Moral values are the topic of the final chapter of this book; for now, it's enough to say that, for most of us, basic moral values are the kinds of things we need to have in common with our friends. When we discover that a friend wants to lie his way to a promotion at work, or torture animals on the weekend, or give money to a white supremacist group, we can't be humble about our differences. Even from the point of view of your own values, the cost of tolerating evil goals is too high. Interference—or at least protest—is warranted here, just as it is in the case of self-destructive values, although the more likely outcome is a dissolution of the friendship.

If we care about other people and we want what's best for them, we should have some humility about our ability to know what it's like for them. This humility doesn't extend so far that we should sit by and watch a friend destroy their own life or act contrary to our most precious values. When it comes to cultivating virtues like humility, Aristotle had good advice. He thought that virtuous states exist at the mean between two extremes and that we should aim for the side that will correct our natural tendency. For example, virtuous humility is in the middle between arrogance and meekness or self-abnegation. If you're a person who inclines toward arrogance, you probably have to work more on not thinking you know everything; if you're inclined to be meek, you may need to work harder on seeing that there are limits to what you should tolerate in other people.

VULNERABILITY

We've seen in this chapter the ways in which many of our values depend on other people. Because other people are mortal creatures with their own ideas, this makes us vulnerable. The people we love sometimes get sick and die or leave us alone. When it comes to valuing people, it's not possible (or desirable) to reinterpret the value as something/someone else. Imagine if my husband died and I thought to myself, "well, what I really valued was an intimate relationship, so I'll just find a new husband, and all will be well." I may value the kind of relationship we have, but I certainly also value *him*—and that's not something that can be seen in a different way.

The Ancient Stoic philosophers thought that we could train ourselves out of this kind of vulnerability:

> With regard to whatever objects give you delight, are useful, or are deeply loved, remember to tell yourself of what general nature they are, beginning from the most insignificant things. If, for example, you are fond of a specific ceramic cup, remind yourself that it is only ceramic cups in general of which you are fond. Then, if it breaks, you will not be disturbed. If you kiss your child, or your wife, say that you only kiss things which are human, and thus you will not be disturbed if either of them dies.[5]

This is an option, I guess. And a really good option when it comes to ceramic cups and other instrumentally valuable things. But when it comes to our attachments to other people, I'm not sure it's possible for most of us to train ourselves in this way. It also doesn't seem like a good thing, even if we could do it. Think about it in goal fulfillment terms: when you love someone, many of your goals are dependent on their existence. If they die, you experience a ton of goal frustration, which is just painful. That is a very unromantic way of thinking about grief, but it does illustrate why we can't really have love without the possibility of grief. For me, I'd rather live a life in which I risk devastating grief, but also feel overwhelming love.

What can we do about our vulnerability, then? The short answer is not much. It's part of the human condition. The flip side of being the kind of creature who can have lasting friendships, loving families, mutual compassion, and extensive cooperation is that we are vulnerable to feelings of grief and deep sadness when the ties between us are severed. But the value perspective does have a strategy to recommend for coping with this reality, which is to cultivate some values that are not so vulnerable so that we have something that gives shape and purpose to life when relationships are threatened.

What makes a value less vulnerable? You might think, given what I just said about human mortality and death, that values with no human connection are the invulnerable ones. But we've just been talking about how almost all of our values involve other people in some way or other. You might find some values that do not depend on other people at all—developing a Stoic attitude toward life might be one of these—but I don't think this will get us very far. Instead, I think we can try to cope with our vulnerability by having some values that depend on people but not on *specific* people. In many areas of life, we can think of ourselves as part of a team or community or institution that is pursuing a valuable project. We may be contributing, with other people, to art, medicine, education, knowledge, religious tradition, justice, human progress, or the like—all things we can identify as values that involve other people, but that transcend the lives of any particular person. We can also think of "being good to others" as a value that makes our lives worth living in a way that is open to the "others" being different people at different times. Such values cannot substitute for the particular other people we love; valuing art, or science, or human progress will not protect us from grief. But these values may give us something to hold on to when our other loves are threatened.

Joe Biden, the president of the United States as I'm writing, is a good example of someone who has done this. As most people know, President Biden suffered tremendous losses in his life, including the deaths of his first wife and young daughter in a car crash and his son Beau to brain cancer. One of the themes of his memoir is the way in which having a sense of a larger purpose helped him to cope with grief and loss. Reflecting on the time of his son's diagnosis, Biden writes:

No matter what came at me, I held fast to my own sense of purpose. I held on for dear life. If I lost hold of that and let Beau's battle consume me, I feared my whole world would collapse. I did not want to let down the country, the Obama administration, my family, myself, or most important, my Beau.[6]

As this quote suggests, valuing something (like the country or a political mission) that transcends particular people does not take away the pain of losing someone we love, but it may give us something to live for until our natural motivations to seek out new values return.

The idea of valuing "being good to others" or contributing to human progress brings us to the topic of moral values. Moral values such as justice, respect, and kindness are vulnerable too, in a way, because many morally bad things happen in this world that are completely out of our control. But in another sense, they are not vulnerable. The nice thing about moral values is that we can pretty much always contribute to them in small ways. We can treat our coworkers with respect, we can contribute to charities that help people in need, we can be kind to flight attendants and baristas, and so on. In so many areas of life, we can choose to put a drop in the bucket and make the world a tiny bit better.

8

FULFILLING OUR
VALUES . . . MORALLY

Moral values and moral obligations are typically characterized by impartiality; the moral community is much larger than
our circle of loved ones. So far, our discussion has been about
what's good for you, me, and our friends and family, but not
what's good for all of us humans (or maybe even all of us
sentient beings). Philosophers have often thought that these
two points of view—partial self-interest and impartial
morality—are two opposing forces, and I've been focused on
the former. Is there anything to say about moral values without violating my promise not to tell you what you *must* value?
I think there is, but before I turn to what can be said, I want
to set the stage by providing a little background about moral
philosophy and this idea of two opposing forces.

WHAT IF NO ONE SEES YOU DO IT?

Imagine you see an attractive ring in an antique shop window.
You're drawn to it and it fits perfectly, so you buy it. When you
get home, you put the ring on your finger and look in the mirror,

and as you twist the ring around, your image disappears. This is, of course, very shocking, so you try it again and again, to confirm that this is actually happening. You wonder if this weird effect is confined to the mirror, so you go outside with the ring turned to make you invisible, and you jump up and down in front of some neighbors. They don't see you (or, apparently, your clothes). You have purchased a magic ring that makes you invisible!

Your mind reels with the possibilities! If you're like my Introduction to Ethics students, the first thing you're going to do is hop on plane to have a free vacation (though they are often caught up by the question of where they'll sit). Second in popularity in the list of new opportunities is to hear what other people are saying about them, but many of them recognize that this might actually be a terrible idea. There's always one student who wants to assassinate an evil person. In general, my students regard it as a fun thing to think about, along the lines of "who would win in a fight: Batman or Spiderman?"

Yet this thought experiment has had a profound role in the history of moral philosophy. In Plato's dialogue *The Republic*, Socrates' interlocutor, Glaucon, introduces the Ring of Gyges (the invisibility ring) as a thought experiment to get Socrates to see that the conflict between self-interest and morality can be resolved only by force. We are selfish creatures, Glaucon posits, and if we weren't worried about getting caught and punished, we would do all manner of horrible things. If we were invisible, the conflict between what's good for us and what's ethical would always be resolved in favor of ourselves. If invisible, we would rape, murder, and steal, because there would be no reason not to.

You can see the history of moral philosophy as an extended dialogue about how to resolve this conflict between self-interest and morality. One major divide in this dialogue is between those who think that the force of morality comes from outside—that we each have our own interests and those interests must be compelled to bend to the moral rules by some outside force like the state or God. This was Glaucon's view, which is why he thought that if we could escape those external forces by being invisible, we would forget about morality completely. The seventeenth-century philosopher Thomas Hobbes was also on this side of the debate. He thought the conflict between self-interest and morality could only be resolved by the force of a dictator, because we humans are too selfish to act nicely without being compelled. These ideas are common to contemporary mainstream economics, according to which "rational economic man" is primarily selfish, and to get him to play nicely we have to punish or pay.

On the other side, we have philosophers who think the force of morality has to come from inside. The eighteenth-century Enlightenment philosopher Immanuel Kant thought the conflict could be resolved by appeal to our own rationality. Moral principles are rational principles, according to Kant, and anyone who is a rational person must recognize the force of them. Others thought that the internal force of morality comes from our sentiments. John Stuart Mill, the social reformer and father of Utilitarianism, believed we resolve the conflict between self-interest and morality by cultivating our sympathy and training our desires so that we care almost as much about other people's happiness as we do about our own.

Scottish philosopher David Hume also thought that our sentiments were crucial to moral values, especially sympathy, which he thought was a wide-ranging, powerful force in human nature:

> A violent cough in another gives us uneasiness; tho' in itself it does not in the least affect us. A man will be mortified, if you tell him he has a stinking breath; tho' 'tis evidently no annoyance to himself. Our fancy easily changes its situation; and either surveying ourselves as we appear to others, or considering others as they feel themselves, makes us enter, by that means, into sentiments, which no way belong to us, and in which nothing but sympathy is able to interest us. And this sympathy we sometimes carry so far, as even to be displeas'd with a quality commodious to us, merely because it displeases others, and renders us disagreeable in their eyes.[1]

Hume thought that sympathy with our fellow humans was the animating principle for all of our judgments about what has value. It's not just that we love our friends and families (which we do), but also that our social nature is inseparable from the very way that we perceive value in the world. When we make judgments about what is good or bad, right or wrong, virtuous or vicious, according to Hume, we take up a point of view from which we sympathize with the interests of other people, whether it's their interest in avoiding our stinky breath or in our treating them with kindness.

In this very old debate, I'm most aligned with David Hume and John Stuart Mill. I think that *all* of our values, including our moral values, are sustained by feelings, not by external forces or the force of rational principles. One problem with relying on our feelings to enforce moral values is that they don't force everyone in the same way. Hobbes's dictator punishes *everyone* for breaking the moral rules, not just people who care about the rules. Kant's rational principles apply to everyone who is minimally capable of logical reasoning. If moral values are backed up by our feelings, then there isn't going to be any argument to compel absolutely everyone to take moral values seriously.

Is this a problem? I guess it would be nice to have a big stick to beat immoral people with. And I'm not the only one who thinks it would be nice. Many of my students want a stick. They come into my Introduction to Ethics class looking for an argument that will destroy the immoral person, bring him to his knees in repentance of his immoral ways. Many of these students, having been raised with some formal religion, assume that such an argument is the point of philosophy. Many of these same students, having been introduced to the reality of cultural differences in their first semester of university, are skeptical that such an argument can be found. From religion, they learn that morality is supposed to be backed up by something absolute that everyone has to accept, and from exposure to groups of people who are different from them, they learn that there isn't any such thing. They put these two lessons together and conclude that morality is a hoax and that, therefore, morally speaking, anything goes.

Absolute absolutism and unqualified relativism are on the menu in moral philosophy. But these are not the only options and they are not the most popular. There is plenty of middle ground where moral values are sustained by human beings and our human practices, and are nevertheless worthy of our commitment. Here, there isn't anything that forces everyone to adopt the same moral values, but there are reasons why most of us do. There's no big cosmic punishment for immorality, but moral values are generally good for us, given what we are like. This middle ground is the ground I think we actually have to stand on.

If that's where we are, let's look on the bright side of it. The bright side starts with the observation that most people do have moral values, despite the lack of an enforcer or a knock-down argument. I see this in my students. No matter how much they cling to skeptical views in conversation, they are (for the most part) good, honest people who volunteer for charity, try a vegan diet because they care about animals, and call their parents even when they don't want to. It turns out their skepticism is only skin deep. And this isn't just true of my students. To see this, we can return to Glaucon and his ring.

Glaucon thought the ring would profoundly alter the bearer's life by eliminating what he saw as life's major conflict: the one between self-interest and morality. But does this seem true? After you stop jumping around in front of your neighbors and return from visiting Paris or the Galapagos, then what? Will your newfound ring help you with the major challenges and conflicts confronting you? Will it help with work/life balance? Will it help you overcome family pressures to be a certain way, or sexist stereotypes that influence how you even conceive of your values? When I think about the challenges that most affect how my life goes, I think of things like this: How do I manage my type 1 diabetes without becoming completely neurotic and no fun? How do I maintain relationships with the people I love who live far away? How can I be a good philosopher without sacrificing some of the qualities I have that don't fit the model of a professional philosopher?

Being invisible would not help me deal with any of these challenges. It wouldn't help me figure out what to value or how much to value it compared with other things. It wouldn't help me figure out when I should give something up because it's too costly in terms of other things I care about, and it wouldn't help me understand what it means to live up to the values that I have. It's fun to think about how we would live if we could get away with anything, but the conflict between selfish interests and the interests of other people is not the conflict that has been central to my life or the lives of the people I know.

Now let's add moral values to the mix. I have some, and likely so do you. We don't need a moral theory to tell us what they are. We can just go with a rough-and-ready list that includes such things as justice, equality, respect, kindness, compassion, and honesty. These are on my list and probably your moral values are similar. Now, are my moral values profoundly different from the other values in my life? They do raise different quandaries for me than the ones I listed a few paragraphs ago. What can I do about racial injustice and disenfranchisement? What kind of volunteering am I capable of that would be meaningful? Am I doing enough? Which charities should I support financially and how much should I give? But in other ways, from my point of view, my moral values aren't fundamentally different from my other values. Notice also, that many of my "non-moral" values are tinged with moral ideals. I want to be a good friend, which means a compassionate friend. I want to be a good teacher, which I think means being fair and honest. There's not even a neat line between our moral goals and our "self-interested" goals.

The invisibility ring is supposed to solve the conflict between self-interest and morality, but if I think about having it, I don't see how it helps me in the moral domain, either. These values aren't going to go away if I put on the ring, after all. I'm still going to care about justice and equality. I'm still going to be concerned with not hurting and disrespecting other people. There can certainly still be a conflict—as there can be conflicts between many of our other values—but it's not a conflict that can be solved by the ability to get away with murder.

All this assumes that I am talking to people who have their own moral values. Rest assured; I am not so naive as to think that this describes everyone. At this moment in history, when people are refusing to wear lightweight face masks to protect others from a deadly virus, it would be crazy to say that everyone cares about justice, respect, and kindness. We also know that digital anonymity on blogs and social media (the twenty-first-century Ring of Gyges) makes some people behave like monsters (trolls, to be exact). Sadly, there are people who actually don't care one bit about other people. I suspect this is true of certain politicians, to the great detriment of us all.

Selfish, immoral jerks are a problem. The problem most relevant to our topic is that their apparently carefree existence might call into doubt our own values. If there are people out there doing just fine without being constrained by the moral values that the rest of us have, this might make us think that we are just suckers. This is really just an extension of the problem Glaucon was worried about: if other people can get away with being immoral, then those of us who follow the rules are suckers! And that's why, in Glaucon's way of thinking, we need to make sure immoral people are punished. If immoral people aren't punished, we might as well be immoral, because it's better than being a sucker. If we think about it, though, how does the fact that someone else doesn't care about other people give *me* a reason not to care about other people? Why do we care about other people? I care about them because I think they are similar to me in important ways, because I sympathize with them, and because I acknowledge that human life would be terrible if it weren't for friendship and community. The fact that there are people who don't care doesn't change any of this. It just isn't true, for most of us, that the only reason we care about treating others with justice, kindness, and respect is that we're afraid of being punished if we don't. And this means that the fact that bad people can get away with it isn't a reason to change our values.

This is what I tell those students who enter the ethics class thinking that the point of it is to find the big argumentative stick. Instead of talking them out of their "you do you" moral relativism, I ask them how it would change how they are living their lives even if it were true.[2] If someone else thinks lying on a job application is perfectly fine, what does that mean for what *you* think is morally OK? What do you think is wrong with lying on job applications? Does that change if there are a few bad eggs who think there's nothing wrong with it? Similarly, if it were OK to kill innocent people in another culture, what would that mean for your life? I try to show them that even if there's no argument for an absolute morality, it doesn't get you out of the hard business of thinking about what matters to you and trying to act consistently with your values.

The remaining problems with selfish, immoral jerks are political problems that really aren't the focus of this book. Selfish jerks make life difficult for the rest of us. They have to be identified and controlled so that they don't wreak havoc. If they are not *total* selfish jerks, they can be persuaded to do better (or at least to follow the basic rules), but people who do not care about others in the slightest need to be forced to follow rules that make life tolerable for everyone else, or they need to be controlled. This is not (as Glaucon would have it) to make sense of morality for the rest of us—it already makes sense to the rest of us! Total selfish jerks, like violent psychopaths, need to be controlled so that the rest of us can pursue our values in peace.

The important thing is that most of us are not selfish jerks. We care about other people, we have moral commitments to them, and we value being this way for reasons that are not undermined by the existence of those who reject these values. The rest of this chapter is unapologetically addressed to those of us who are not selfish jerks. I'll assume a set of values we share: the other-focused values that include helpfulness, justice, respect, and honesty. And I'll ask what happens when we look at these values through the lens of resolving the conflicts between our goals and pursuing our own values. The first thing we notice is that there's actually a lot of harmony already.

MORAL VALUES AND HARMONY

In chapter 7, we saw how our values are intertwined with other people we care about—friends, teammates, community members. It should not surprise you to find out that moral values also tend to be well integrated into our systems of values. Before we get into the details, a few caveats. First, this is a book about how to live your own life well by identifying your values and resolving conflicts among your goals and between your goals and the world. It's not a book about morality and I'm not coming from the perspective of any specific moral theory. I'm going to talk about some moral values that most of us share in the same way that I talked about the values of career and family. We may all have somewhat different ways of interpreting values such as justice, respect, and kindness, but there's some core that makes it sensible to speak about our valuing the same things.

Even without assuming a grand moral theory, we can use the values perspective in this book to help us characterize our moral values. In other words, the value fulfillment approach taken in this book can illuminate our moral values, even if it doesn't really tell us what to value from the moral point of view. For example, if we think about helpfulness from the standpoint of our goal-seeking nature, we can see that we help people by enabling them to fulfill their values and to resolve their conflicts. Justice, in this way of thinking, requires (among other things) that everyone be free of the kind of deprivation, fear, and insecurity that make it impossible to do what matters to them. Respect requires that we take seriously other people's capacities to make decisions about what matters. In turn, it requires being honest with others so that they can make their decisions on the basis of good information.

If we take other people into consideration in our moral point of view, we should care about whether they are able to identify, modify, and pursue their own values. We should care about whether they have the basic necessities of life, without which it's not possible to think about much of anything except getting those necessities. We should care about legal, economic, and social obstacles to people's ability to do the things that matter to them. The idea that it's good for people to fulfill their most important values informs how we think about what helpfulness, justice, and respect require. This is far from a moral theory, but it does provide one way of filling in some details about these moral values. Moreover, it's a way of filling in details that dovetails nicely with how we think about our own lives.

The second caveat is that my way of talking about moral values may sound very individualistic and specific to my own culture. I start with the idea that morality is basically about enabling people to pursue their own goals. That sounds very Western. I do anticipate that most of my readers are from Western cultures, so that's part of it. But I also want to point out that this focus on goal-seeking is not individualistic in an objectionable sense, because people's goals can be social. In cultures that emphasize community over individual achievement, people may have goals that are more attuned to their communal and familial obligations, or to their place in the group; their values may be informed by other people's values to a greater extent than is true for people who live in more individualistic cultures. Helping such people may require greater attention to the group than to the individual. But this doesn't mean that moral values point in a completely different direction for less individualistic cultures.

Indeed, as we'll see, I'm inclined to think that even those of us who live in Western cultures have many values that are fundamentally social. So, the individualist appearance of what I'm saying about moral values is superficial. This makes sense, because, as we have seen throughout this book, people's individual values are dependent on other people in all sorts of ways. Helping another person to pursue her values, or helping to ensure that everyone has the ability to pursue their values, will naturally require that we think about how people are connected to each other. To put it simply, we are social creatures, and to help a social individual you have to help the others on whom they depend.

With those caveats out of the way, let's consider the question: how do our moral values harmonize with our other values?

The first thing to notice is that our own ability to pursue our personal goals—careers, friendships, hobbies—depends on our living in communities that are governed by certain standards of behavior. We need people to be basically moral and decent in order to succeed, because so much of what we do depends on coordinating with others. Basic moral decency includes generally telling the truth, sticking to agreements, not assaulting or injuring each other, not stealing each other's stuff, and helping each other out when we're in need. From the point of view of one venerable moral theory, social contract theory, this point about our dependence on each other's decency is at the very center of morality. According to social contract theory, the right moral rules are the ones everyone would agree to, if they were thinking clearly. The idea behind this theory is that we cannot survive, let alone thrive, without cooperation, and so (if we're being reasonable) we would all agree to some basic moral rules to govern us. Life without these basic rules would be, as Hobbes famously put it, "solitary, poor, nasty, brutish, and short." Such a life would be bad for fulfilling your values, unless the only thing you valued was hunkering down in a bunker with your guns.

In order to fulfill our own values, we need to trust others to be basically morally decent. This fact has a lot to do with how we end up *valuing* basic moral decency. We've evolved to find these moral values appealing and we're taught them very early in childhood. Children as young as eighteen months seem to like people who are nice and shun people who are mean.[3] Human life wouldn't work if we all grew up to be psychopaths, and so we do not. Instead, moral values develop naturally and become central to our identities. Because we need them, moral values are not weeds.

The second thing to notice is that moral values are often intertwined with specific personal goals. We can see this with career goals, in that many professions have ethical codes. For example, health care professionals' career goals are constrained by moral imperatives such as "do no harm" in the Hippocratic Oath. Teachers aim to help students, and not just the ones they like. Lawyers take an oath to serve their clients in accordance with duty. My grandfather, a businessman, prided himself on his honest dealings with others and the fact that even his competitors could trust his word.

Another way in which personal and moral values are entwined comes from people who face obstacles to achieving their own goals from social injustice (as discussed in chapter 5). For someone in this situation, combating injustice can be at the same time a moral project and a self-affirming or self-respecting project. These moral and personal goals sometimes interact in subtle ways. Consider how sexism and other forms of oppression can be self-sustaining by making their victims feel less capable of doing what they want to do. Imposter syndrome, which makes us doubt our abilities and feel like frauds, can frustrate our goals by diverting our energy to worrying and preventing us from taking risks. Imposter syndrome can also frustrate our *moral* values. For example, I think that the experience of feeling like an imposter in philosophy had the effect of making me believe I had no power to help people, including my own students. I'm sure I'm not alone in this feeling. If you feel like a student, you're not likely to see yourself as a teacher; if you feel like an apprentice, you're not likely to be a mentor; if you feel like a subordinate, you're not likely to take on the role of a boss. So, I spent quite a few years not being much of a mentor to my students, or at least not the kind of mentor I have seen my male colleagues be or the kind I would have liked to be. I was too busy feeling I needed help to be helpful to others.

This feature of sexism makes it all the more motivating to think about directing one's energy into fighting the structures that have hindered you. Working against sexism helps me achieve my moral value of justice and also helps me to see myself as powerful and capable of helping others. It even has potential effects that would benefit my goal of making room for the kind of philosophy I think is worthwhile. In this case, moral values and personal goals are very much mixed up together. My desire to help my students is partly a professional and partly a moral goal. My interest in combating sexism is partly moral, but also partly personal. For people who are directly affected by injustice, working against injustice probably doesn't fit neatly in one (moral or not-moral) bucket.

One last example of how moral values and particular personal values are intertwined has to do with the psychological benefits of helping others. There's good evidence that people who are helpful to others actually feel happier than people who aren't.[4] Expressing gratitude to and helping other people by choice tends to increase our positive emotions and our feelings of satisfaction with our lives. Even when helpfulness costs you, it makes you happier. For example, in one study, researchers rated experiment participants' happiness before getting a "windfall" ($5 or $20), which half of them were instructed to spend on themselves (the "personal spending group") and half were instructed to spend on others (the "prosocial spending group") by 5:00 that afternoon. At the end of the day, the participants' happiness was assessed again, and it turned out that those who spent the money on other people were happier than the ones who spent it on themselves.[5] I don't find this research terribly surprising. I think Hume was correct about our human nature: we are sympathetic creatures who can't help but care how we are regarded by our fellow human beings. Of course doing things that make other people like us makes us feel good!

Now the question is how best to make use of this research in our lives. Psychologist Sonja Lyubomirsky recommends "happiness interventions" such as performing random acts of kindness and writing gratitude letters.[6] This isn't bad advice, but it's up to us to figure out how to follow it. An interesting finding from this research (which tends to get less attention than the basic news that altruism makes us happy) is that the happiness benefits of helping others accrue to people who freely choose to benefit others, not to those who are pressured into doing it.[7] In other words, benefiting others has to be connected to our own goals if it's going to make us feel good. We are better off finding ways to help others that are guided by our own values and compatible with our other goals.

The psychological research on happiness and helpfulness is focused on positive feelings and life satisfaction, because this is how psychologists in this field tend to measure well-being. But there is another positive feeling that arises from helping others: the feeling of confidence that we're on the right path. When we are anxious about the conflicts we're experiencing and unsure how to resolve them—and especially if these anxieties veer into a crisis about our values—other-focused moral values are helpful. It's the rare soul who gets to the end of life and says regretfully, "I spent too much time being nice to people" or "I wish I hadn't been so fair and helpful to my fellow humans." To return to our gardening metaphor, if you're looking for a hardy and attractive plant, moral values are an excellent choice. Moral values and prosocial actions are like plants that always look good, no matter the season.

Being helpful contributes to the personal goal of being happy and secure. Fighting for justice can give us the confidence we need to be ambitious in other goals. Being honest contributes to our having satisfying careers. Acting on our moral values can serve more than one of our values at a time. Notice how far we have come from the picture of human nature that Glaucon assumes, where our biggest problem is how to avoid having to sacrifice anything for another person. In fact, much of what we do for others is no sacrifice, and very often when we do have to make sacrifices it's because of values and principles we care about deeply. Our biggest problem is how to uphold all of the competing values we have, including so many values that are inseparable from morality.

MORAL VALUES AND DISCORD

Most of us do have moral values that direct us to help other people and to treat them fairly and with respect. And most of us have many different motivations to act on these values, including some that have to do with our personal projects. There is a lot more harmony to humanity than Glaucon and Hobbes thought. However, it's hard to deny that there is also conflict. What do we do when moral values conflict with our other values and goals?

It will help to be specific about the kind of conflict we're wondering about. Let's focus first on the one between our positive moral obligations to help make the world a better place—a place in which more people are able to pursue what matters to them—and our other goals. I think most people who have moral values do want to "make a contribution" or "leave the world a better place than it was when they found it"; these are common moral aspirations. I'm calling these our "positive" moral obligations, because they are obligations to *do* something (like giving to others)—as opposed to obligations to refrain from doing something (like lying or stealing). Making the world a better place in any significant way, however, is really demanding.

We live in a world where twelve million children live in food-insecure households in the United States (the richest country in the world), millions of children in poor countries are suffering from easily curable diseases, and climate change is on course to make everything so much worse.[8] As I write this in 2022, we have just lived through a moment in which the injustice of racism and poverty have been vividly illustrated. At this minute, the injustice and cruelty of war is on terrible display in Ukraine. Some of the events have been so disheartening, so awful, that I find myself, along with many others I know, in a situation in which my moral values demand more of me than I can handle. To really go for it, we'd have to work on this goal every waking minute. That would conflict with many of the other things we want to do. According to one strain of the Utilitarian philosophical tradition, sacrificing everything for morality is the right thing to do.[9] Utilitarianism says that the right action is the one that produces the greatest happiness for the greatest number. If we think in this way, the moral value of helping others not to suffer will conflict with all of our other goals. I could do more to alleviate suffering if I gave up lots of other things that are, from the moral point of view, less important. I am 100 percent certain that I could do more good for the world by *not* learning to play the ukulele.

How do we resolve this conflict? If we think back to our strategy in chapter 4 for dealing with conflicts, one question we can ask ourselves is whether one of the goals or values should be abandoned. Given all the ways that our moral values are integrated into our systems of values (the subject of the previous section), giving up our moral values is not a good option. They aren't weeds. What about the other way? Why not give up all of our other goals and become a kind of moral superstar? The problem with this strategy is that even if it is the right thing to do from the moral point of view, I don't think most of us could do it. This is true for the same reason that we can't give up our moral values: many of the things we care about that take time away from improving the world are things that are central to the system of values we identify with. Friendship, family, career, art, sports, faith—these are not weeds either.

If we're stuck with the conflict, we have to think about changing the means to our ends or reinterpreting the end. Changing the means to the end of "being moral" or "making the world a better place" isn't going to help us very much, because part of the problem is that we're not quite sure what this requires. So, we would do well to think about our reinterpretation strategy. Is there a way of thinking about the value of making the world a better place that reduces the conflict between morality and our other goals? I think so—we can think of our moral values in terms of doing our fair share as part of a team or moral community. I'm not saying that *do your fair share* is *the* right way to think about moral values if we are focused on what is morally required. Maybe from the moral point of view, this is not enough. But *do your fair share* is a way to think about morality that is useful for all of us who are struggling to figure out how to juggle multiple goals and demands on our time.

Also, *do your fair share* does have deep roots in moral philosophy. It is the strategy recommended by at least two long-standing traditions: rule utilitarianism and social contract theory.[10] Both of these would recommend that we identify and follow some rules for our moral contributions—rules that govern how much of our time we should devote to helping other people, how much money we should donate to worthy causes, and so on. Rule utilitarianism says that the right rules are the ones that would produce the best results if everyone were to follow them. Social contract theory, as described earlier, says that the right rules are the ones we would all agree on if we had a reasonable and fair discussion about how to conduct our lives together. Either way, these rules don't demand huge sacrifice, because they are defined against the background assumption that we're all in this together and each of us needs to follow the same rules. If we think of our moral values this way, instead of thinking that our contributions are only important if they are big, we can think that we're doing pretty well, morally speaking, as long as we do our part.

Do your fair share has a good philosophical pedigree, but it also has some problems.

The biggest problem is that, of course, not everyone does their part. The moral rules it makes sense to follow are the ones that work if we all follow them. They are the rules that assume we are equal players on the moral team. But this is obviously false, and "Let's all pitch in and do our part!" might sound seriously naive. There are moral superstars who do much more than the rest of us to alleviate suffering and fight for justice. There are people who devote their lives to political activism, people who donate kidneys to strangers, people who take jobs in finance so that they can donate more money to effective charities.[11] There are also moral monsters who make everything dramatically worse for everyone else. And then there are plenty of shirkers who aren't committing genocide or fomenting the overthrow of democracy, but who are not particularly helpful and not particularly committed to justice.

It would be a wonderful world if we all did our part. If we were all rowing the boat in the same direction, we'd get to our destination with ease. Instead, we have people rowing in different directions and some people taking sniper shots at other rowers. What does this mean for the *do your fair share* program? Well, it is true that most of us are capable of responding to short-term moral emergencies by dropping everything else and putting all of our energy into rowing us away from disaster. After George Floyd's murder by a Minneapolis police officer, and in the last days of the Trump administration when it seemed that our democracy was on the brink of failure, many Americans did much more than they normally do. People went to rallies and protests despite a pandemic, wrote checks to antiracist groups and organizations that supported fair voting, volunteered for get-out-the-vote organizations and food pantries, and so on. But most people aren't capable of living in emergency mode forever. For nonemergency times, doing your part is better than doing nothing, and doing your part might be all most of us are really able to do. (Maybe I'm selling human beings short here, but I don't think so.)

This emphasis on what we're able to do raises another concern. It might seem like *do your fair share* makes it possible for us to fulfill our moral values by lowering the bar. This reminds me of the saying that the secret to good self-esteem is to lower your standards to the point at which they're already met. Am I suggesting that we lower our moral standards? That doesn't seem right, and it isn't what I mean. There's a difference between seeing yourself as playing a small role in an ambitious project and seeing yourself as playing the leading role in a meager project. My suggestion is that we maintain very high standards for what would make the world a better place, but acknowledge that those standards can only be met by many people working together. The standards for *my* actions are the standards for a team player, not a superstar.

But you might still worry that this lets human beings off the hook too easily. If we think of ourselves as moral "team players," won't we settle for a pretty low personal bar, even if we keep the bar for the team high? Not necessarily. First, being on a team often makes us play better. As sympathetic creatures, we want to impress other people and make them think well of us. We don't want to let others down, and we are motivated by their example.

Second, as with many of our values, moral values bring along with them aspirational commitments to improvement. John Rawls, one of the great philosophers of the twentieth century, called this the Aristotelian principle, writing, "Human beings enjoy the exercise of their realized capacities (their innate or trained abilities), and this enjoyment increases the more the capacity is realized, or the greater its complexity."[12] This idea that we get more out of our activities when we take on more challenges and improve is also supported by psychological science. The research on "flow experiences" (discussed in chapter 3) shows that there is a sweet spot for flow between boredom and anxiety, the point at which a person is challenged enough to be excited, but not so much as to be frustrated.[13] As our skills develop, this spot moves forward. So, as with any of our important values, we shouldn't get complacent.

To avoid complacency, we can think about improving or doing better than we have in the past. As might be guessed by the name of Rawls' principle, Aristotle was a fan of self-improvement. He recommended a program of character development in which we model ourselves after people who are better than we are, acting consistently with virtue until we become the kind of people to whom it comes naturally. "Fake it 'til you make it" is the slogan my students think of when they are introduced to Aristotle. Now, for Aristotle, being virtuous meant being guided by our rational faculties and achieving moderation in our passions and desires; it didn't have specifically to do with alleviating suffering or global poverty. But his basic idea that we can commit ourselves to being better people is a good way of thinking about the moral values we have now. We can do our fair share while being on the lookout for ways in which we could be doing better. Again, this is not so different from how it is with many of our goals. For most of our complex activities, the ideal of improvement is built in. This means that thinking of our moral values as recommending that we do our fair share does not mean that we'll just kick back and acquiesce in a mediocre performance. (We may do this, of course, out of laziness or selfishness, but it's not the fault of *do your fair share!*)

Some practical advice about morality arises from thinking that we should do our fair share without becoming complacent: Do something. Do something that fits you and your life. Do something that fits long term.

"Do something" is pretty straightforward. "Do something that fits you and your life" is not so different from good advice for any of our goals. And, as we've seen with other goals, what fits you and your life depends a lot on the details and can mean different things for different people.[14] Some people need some variety in their lives and might benefit from fulfilling their moral values in a way that lets them do something completely different. Some people have too much on their plates and would be best suited to contributing to their moral values concurrently with other goals—for example, spending more time with their children by doing volunteer work together. Also, as with other goals, what fits long term needn't be exactly the same thing forever. As our lives change and we have more or less time, money, and energy, what fits may also change. Moral emergencies will arise that demand more attention in the short term. But for the long term, we are well served by finding ways to make the world a better place that don't end up exhausting us in a matter of months.

As we saw in chapter 5, the social context in which we try to fulfill our values can create challenges for us. For example, being on the receiving end of racist or gender bias may make a person more motivated to work on these problems, potentially allowing them to achieve personal and moral goals at the same time. On one hand, this can be a good thing. Directing your "make the world a better place" resources to something that is personally meaningful is a good way to do something that fits you for the long term. On the other hand, it's unfair that the people who are most harmed by oppression are the ones spending the most time fixing it. Recognizing this can be discouraging and can even create resentment. Resentment is toxic for value fulfillment, because it turns us toward ruminating on the unfairness, or punishing the people who benefit from it, which doesn't usually help us do what really matters to us. Just as with our other goals and values, it helps to understand the context in which we are trying to pursue our moral goals and to take this into account as we navigate a way to fit our values together.

So far, I've focused on positive moral obligations to help others, improve the world, work for justice, and so on. What about negative moral obligations such as the obligations not to lie or steal or kill innocent people? *Do your fair share but don't get complacent* doesn't cut it here. Your fair share of not killing innocent people is, well, never killing an innocent person. And stealing *less* than you did last year isn't morally very good at all. Kant called these moral duties "perfect," by which he meant that they are duties we must always perform. We have no discretion here in how we interpret the moral value. I suspect there isn't perfect consensus about this—many people think that little white lies are morally OK, for example. But there is widespread agreement that these negative moral obligations are much more strict than the positive obligation to make the world a better place.

Because of that agreement, I think the right way to think about these obligations when it comes to value fulfillment and goal conflict is to think of them as constraints rather than goals. Refraining from lying to advance your own goals is not itself a goal that should be fit together with the rest of them. Refraining from murdering the colleague who stands in the way of your promotion is not a goal that you should try to re-interpret so that it's compatible with your values. These "thou shalt not" moral rules are the limits on what we should do in pursuit of our goals and values. To return to our gardening metaphor, they're like the boundaries of our property. As you're planning your garden, you shouldn't even consider planting things in your neighbor's yard (even if they have more sun for your roses).

———

Glaucon isn't wrong that morality and self-interest conflict. But I think he is wrong to say that this is the central conflict of our lives. For most of us, the conflict between "doing the right thing" and "doing what we want" is not the sort that causes a midlife crisis or existential angst, or that drives us to therapy. What causes more trouble for us is how to fit things together, not whether to ditch morality for the sake of selfish pursuits.

When the Existentialist philosopher Jean-Paul Sartre—an expert on the existential crisis, if ever there was one—wants to give an example that illustrates the philosophy of Existentialism, he talks about his student who

> at this moment, had the choice between going to England to join the Free French Forces or of staying near his mother and helping her to live. He fully realised that this woman lived only for him and that his disappearance—or perhaps his death—would plunge her into despair.[15]

Sartre's student was choosing between war and caring for his mother. Neither of these options sounds all that great for him, from the point of view of selfish interests. Each is recommended by a different *moral* value and they are mutually exclusive options. That's the crisis.

For the Existentialist, our moral and other choices are not determined by reason, human nature, or anything else. We are radically free to choose what we want and it is our choice that imbues the option with value. The only constraint on the soldier, from the Existentialist's point of view, is that he should choose "authentically"—that is, he should acknowledge his own freedom and take responsibility for whatever he decides. And yet, as we can see from Sartre's example, even an Existentialist thinks that moral values can be compelling: contrary to egoists like Glaucon, morality is sometimes what we choose.

Obviously, I agree with the Existentialists about this, but I would add that moral values are compelling because of what we human beings are like. So, choice is also vital in my approach, just not *radical* choice. Our choices should be informed by what we're like psychologically, by our circumstances, and by whatever else we take to matter. We don't garden with radical freedom, after all. We have to plant what will grow where we live.

CONCLUSION

I sometimes watch my dogs with envy. They seem to live their lives without much effort. Lying in the sun, watching squirrels, or sitting for a treat, they are "all-in," with no conflict and no doubt about whether they are doing something worthwhile. Because of our complex and reflective minds, this kind of easy contentment eludes many of us. The things that matter to us come into conflict and cause us to wonder whether we're barking up the wrong tree. This has certainly been my experience, and I know it isn't mine alone. Everyone I know wonders what they should do with themselves, whether they're doing the right thing in the right way, and how to improve life for themselves and the people they love.

My solution to this human problem is to figure out what really matters and find ways to live up to those values in your life. But do we really need this philosophical approach? Why not just Google it? You can indeed Google what really matters! It's health, family, friends, love, purpose, passion, and education, many of the things we've been talking about in this book. But I don't think that solves our problem, because we need to know *how* to value these things: What does valuing friendship mean? When work and family conflict, which is more important? How do you find your passion? We have to figure this out as we go—by learning about ourselves and our environment, refining our values and goals, trying things out, and being willing to learn from our experience. In this process, I have found it helpful to think about myself as a goal-seeking creature, the same as any other animal. Like them, I do better when I can achieve the things that matter to me and, also like them, I have goals that are deeply rooted and difficult to change. Unlike them, I'm able to change what matters to me and how I think about it (at least to some extent). The sophisticated human brain that gives rise to the problem also provides the solution by giving us the flexibility to refine our values and to reinterpret what it means to succeed in terms of what really matters.[1]

Thinking about yourself as a goal-seeker can seem individualistic. I have my goals and you have yours, and we each seek to attain them independently. But this appearance of individualism is really just that. Seeking to fulfill your values is only as lonely as the values themselves. We value other people, our relationships with them, the communities we share, and the work we do together. Other people are indispensable for learning about ourselves and for sustaining our sense that what we are doing makes a difference. To find our best values, we should recognize all the ways in which our values connect us to each other. If finding, refining, and pursuing our values is like gardening, not only do we not garden with radical freedom, but we don't garden alone.

The other day, I was talking to some similarly middle-aged friends about how surprising we find it to be as old as we are. My mother and her friends are also surprised by their age. It seems to me that this feeling of surprise has to do with the fact that none of us had the experience we were expecting of everything just settling down. When we were young, we predicted that when we were old we would have figured it all out, we would know what we were doing, we would feel wise and mature. The positive way to describe this is that life is always in process! Though we may have assumed otherwise when we were young, life isn't the kind of thing you figure out and then set to autopilot. We keep moving, setting new goals, encountering new conflicts, and figuring out how to resolve them. If this is our human condition, we are well served by identifying values that illuminate the path and trying to live up to them with commitment and flexibility.

ACKNOWLEDGMENTS

I want to thank my father, Richard Tiberius, for encouraging me to think that the ideas I've been exploring in my academic work on well-being might be of interest to a wider audience. It's worth saying that my dad is not one of those "everything you do is the best!" parents. He's more old school. In response to my first book, his response was, "Well, Val, it's really . . . dense." And in response to the first draft of this book, he hemmed and hawed before telling me that it read like the plan for a graduate seminar. This was obviously not a compliment. But he has been enthusiastic about the improvements and I hope I have done justice to all the wonderfully rewarding conversations we had as the book progressed. As I worked on the manuscript, it became a family affair. My husband, J. D. Walker, my mother, Merike Lugus, and my sister, Paula Tiberius (all of them writers themselves), provided generous feedback and encouragement. All three of these people are a little bit closer to "everything you do is the best!" so their excellent criticisms were delightfully sprinkled with compliments. My mother-in-law, Zella Walker, also gave helpful feedback, which resulted in the addition of the "Roadmap." I am very grateful to my family and also to my friends, without whom I would know much less about what is valuable in life.

I was fortunate to have the insightful and conscientious help of Qiannan Li as my research assistant while working on this book. This good fortune was made possible by the Paul W. Frenzel chair in Liberal Arts. I am so grateful to my editor, Rob Tempio, who thought long ago that I should write a book for a broader audience and who answered my many questions promptly and helpfully while he was sorting out his own value conflicts in lockdown with a small child. The Princeton University Press team has been wonderful to work with. Thanks also to my copyeditor, Katherine Harper, whose help with the manuscript went beyond the call of duty. I also want to thank my two anonymous reviewers, who provided detailed, constructive comments. I owe a particular debt to the anonymous reviewer Dan Haybron, who knows me too well to remain anonymous. Many of his questions on the manuscript resulted in substantial improvements, though I'm sure my approach is still too subjective for his taste. Thanks are also due to Colin DeYoung, who answers all my questions about psychological research with clarity and patience, and to Jemma Rane for her insight into my life and life in general.

It was not my initial plan to write a book that had anything to do with sexism. But as I thought about the disconnect between my own attempts to live a good life and what I read in academic philosophy, it suddenly seemed that this perspective was something I could contribute. I don't think I would have had this thought had it not been for the many young women academics who have responded positively to my work and told me that they appreciate that I talk about practical topics that are usually ignored by mainstream philosophy. Sukaina Hirji deserves particular thanks for her inspiring comments on my previous book. Conversations with my colleagues Juliette Cherbuliez, Jessica Gordon-Roth, and Melissa Koenig also helped me to see the value of this perspective. Because of these women, and the work of feminist philosophers who have always thought it was OK to talk about one's own personal experiences, I was encouraged to include examples from my life. I am grateful to these trailblazing women, and also to those who are following bravely in their footsteps.

NOTES

PREFACE

1. On gratitude practices and other happiness habits, see Sonja Lyubomirsky, *The How of Happiness: A Scientific Approach to Getting the Life You Want* (New York: Penguin Press, 2008), 89–101. You can learn about active constructive responding in many places online, for example: https://positivepsychology.com/active-constructive -communication/.

2. James Baldwin, *Go Tell It on the Mountain* (New York: Knopf Doubleday, 2013); Ta-Nehisi Coates, *The Beautiful Struggle* (London: One World, 2009); Nikole Hannah-Jones, *The 1619 Project: A New Origin Story* (New York: Random House, 2021); Ibram X. Kendi, *How to Be an Antiracist* (London: One World, 2019); Isabel Wilkerson, *The Warmth of Other Suns: The Epic Story of America's Great Migration* (New York: Vintage, 2011).

CHAPTER 1. WHAT WE WANT AND WHAT STANDS IN OUR WAY

1. Princeton University Press recently changed its policies to allow authors to use "they" and "them" as singular, third-person, gender-neutral pronouns. I know it grates on some people's grammatical nerves, but I am with *New York*

Times columnist Farhad Manjoo in thinking that "It's Time for 'They'": https://www.nytimes.com/2019/07/10/opinion/pronoun-they-gender.html.

2. Here are a few contemporary classics from the philosophy literature that represent the diversity of perspectives: Fred Feldman, *Pleasure and the Good Life: Concerning the Nature, Varieties, and Plausibility of Hedonism* (Oxford: Clarendon Press, 2004); Richard Kraut, *What Is Good and Why* (Cambridge, MA: Harvard University Press, 2009); L. W. Sumner, *Welfare, Happiness, and Ethics* (Oxford: Clarendon Press, 1999).

3. The psychology literature is vast. You can get a sense of the variety of perspectives in the research here: Daniel Kahneman, Edward Diener, and Norbert Schwarz, eds. *Well-Being: Foundations of Hedonic Psychology.* (New York: Russell Sage Foundation, 2003); Shane J. Lopez and C. R. Snyder, eds., *Handbook of Positive Psychology* (New York: Oxford University Press, 2011); Alan S. Waterman, ed., *The Best within Us: Positive Psychology Perspectives on Eudaimonia* (Washington, DC: American Psychological Association, 2013).

4. Valerie Tiberius, *Well-Being as Value Fulfillment: How We Can Help Each Other to Live Well* (Oxford: Oxford University Press, 2018).

5. Psychologists have shown that people do rely on these important domains of life to assess their overall life satisfaction. U. Schimmack, E. Diener, and S. Oishi, "Life-Satisfaction Is a Momentary Judgment and a Stable Personality Characteristic: The Use of Chronically Accessible and Stable Sources," in *Assessing Well-Being* (Dordrecht: Springer, 2009), 181–212; William Pavot and Ed Diener,

"The Satisfaction with Life Scale and the Emerging Construct of Life Satisfaction," *The Journal of Positive Psychology* 3, no. 2 (2008): 137–52.

6. There is a sense in which I agree with Existentialism about "human essence," however. I agree that there is no universal human nature that defines what is good for each person independent of that person's choices. Nevertheless, whatever features of human nature an individual person shares will shape what it is good for them to value.

CHAPTER 2. WHAT TURTLES, DOGS, AND PEOPLE HAVE IN COMMON

1. The works that have influenced me the most here are Colin G. DeYoung, "Cybernetic Big Five Theory," *Journal of Research in Personality* 56 (2015): 33–58; and Charles S. Carver and Michael F. Scheier, *On the Self-Regulation of Behavior* (Cambridge: Cambridge University Press, 2001).

2. Working memory is the small percentage of our memory that we can use in conscious reasoning. Most of our memories are stored in long-term memory, which is not immediately accessible. Bernard J. Baars and Stan Franklin, "How Conscious Experience and Working Memory Interact," *Trends in Cognitive Sciences* 7, no. 4 (2003): 166–72.

3. Roy Baumeister and Mark R. Leary, "The Need to Belong: Desire for Interpersonal Attachments as a Fundamental Human Motivation," *Psychological Bulletin* 117, no. 3 (1995): 497.

4. Christine L. Nittrouer et al., "Gender Disparities in Colloquium Speakers at Top Universities," *Proceedings of the*

National Academy of Sciences 115, no. 1 (2017): 104–8; Deborah James and Janice Drakich. "Understanding Gender Differences in Amount of Talk: A Critical Review of Research," in *Gender and Conversational Interaction*, ed. Deborah Tannen (Oxford: Oxford University Press on Demand, 1993), 281–312.

CHAPTER 3. WHAT ARE OUR VALUES . . . AND WHAT SHOULD THEY BE?

1. Two excellent books that review the psychological research are Daniel M. Haybron, *The Pursuit of Unhappiness: The Elusive Psychology of Well-Being* (Oxford: Oxford University Press, 2008) and Timothy D. Wilson, *Strangers to Ourselves: Discovering the Adaptive Unconscious* (Cambridge, MA: Harvard University Press, 2004).

2. Even when she makes these remarks, she's not sure that she is in love; it takes her a little longer to figure that out. Jane Austen, *Pride and Prejudice* (New York: Alfred A. Knopf, 1991), 196.

3. Joni Mitchell, "Big Yellow Taxi," *Ladies of the Canyon*, 1970.

4. Here, I am sympathetic to a theory of practical reason called "specificationism." Henry S. Richardson, *Practical Reasoning about Final Ends* (Cambridge: Cambridge University Press, 1997).

5. Justin Kruger and David Dunning, "Unskilled and Unaware of It: How Difficulties in Recognizing One's Own Incompetence Lead to Inflated Self-Assessments," *Journal of Personality and Social Psychology* 77, no. 6 (1999): 1121; Ola Svenson. "Are We All Less Risky and More Skillful than

Our Fellow Drivers?," *Acta psychologica* 47, no. 2 (1981): 143–48.

6. Abraham Harold Maslow, "A Theory of Human Motivation," *Psychological Review* 50, no. 4 (1943): 370.

7. Carol D. Ryff, "Happiness Is Everything, or Is It? Explorations on the Meaning of Psychological Well-Being," *Journal of Personality and Social Psychology* 57, no. 6 (1989): 1069; Richard M. Ryan and Edward L. Deci, "On Happiness and Human Potentials: A Review of Research on Hedonic and Eudaimonic Well-Being," *Annual Review of Psychology* 52, no. 1 (2001): 141–66.

8. The Occupational Safety and Health Administration (OSHA) in the US Department of Labor lists stress as a workplace hazard because of its effects on health: https://www.osha.gov/etools/hospitals/hospital-wide-hazards/work-related-stress. For a review of some of the research, see Michelle M. Larzelere and Glenn N. Jones, "Stress and Health," *Primary Care: Clinics in Office Practice* 35, no. 4 (2008): 839–56.

9. Gordon Moskowitz and Heidi Grant, eds., *The Psychology of Goals* (New York: Guilford Press, 2009), 480–505.

10. "5 Benefits of Boredom," *Psychology Today,* April 4, 2020, https://www.psychologytoday.com/ca/blog/science-choice/202004/5-benefits-boredom.

11. We should be aware that generalized boredom and lack of interest in normal activities could also be a sign of depression.

12. Daniel M. Haybron, *Happiness: A Very Short Introduction* (Oxford: Oxford University Press, 2013), 21. The original research on flow is due to Mihaly Csikszentmihalyi, *Flow: The Psychology of Optimal Experience* (New York: Harper and Row, 1990).

13. "Waiting Games," *Hidden Brain* podcast with Kyla Rankin, https://hiddenbrain.org/podcast/waiting-games/.

14. Joy and tranquility are the other two components of happiness, according to Haybron, *Happiness*, 23.

15. Michaéla C. Schippers and Niklas Ziegler, "Life Crafting as a Way to Find Purpose and Meaning in Life," *Frontiers in Psychology* 10 (2019): 2778. There are some good online resources for these exercises, and a good personal coach or therapist could probably also recommend some.

16. Simine Vazire. "Who Knows What about a Person? The Self–Other Knowledge Asymmetry (SOKA) Model," *Journal of Personality and Social Psychology* 98, no. 2 (2010): 281.

17. Martin Luther King, Jr., "A Letter from Birmingham Jail." *Ebony* Aug. 1963: 23–32, 25.

18. Kendi, *How to Be an Antiracist*, 6.

19. Play is one of our essential human functions, according to Martha C. Nussbaum, *Women and Human Development: The Capabilities Approach* (New York: Cambridge University Press, 2001), 80.

CHAPTER 4. ON STRAWBERRIES AND SAFETY: OR, HOW TO RESOLVE CONFLICTS

1. LGBTQ people navigate this kind of conflict in different ways. My thinking about this topic has been influenced by reading D. Moon and T. W. Tobin, "Sunsets and Solidarity: Overcoming Sacramental Shame in Conservative Christian Churches to Forge a Queer Vision of Love and Justice," *Hypatia* 33, no. 3 (2018): 451–68; J. E. Sumerau, R. T. Cragun, and L. A. Mathers, "Contemporary Religion

and the Cisgendering of Reality," *Social Currents* 3, no. 3 (2016): 293–311; Mimi Swartz, "Living the Good Lie," *The New York Times*, June 19, 2011, https://www.nytimes.com /2011/06/19/magazine/therapists-who-help-people-stay-in -the-closet.html; John Gustave-Wrathall, "Pillars of My Faith," *Affirmation: LGBTQ Mormons, Family and Friends,* August 16, 2014, https://affirmation.org/pillars-faith/.

2. According to psychologist Mark Snyder, an expert on volunteerism, "A recurring theme in research on volunteerism is that volunteers are more satisfied, effective, and long-serving if their volunteering fulfills their personal and social motivations for serving as volunteers." (Personal conversation, 2021.) See also Mark Snyder, Allen M. Omoto, and P. C. Dwyer, "Volunteerism: Multiple Perspectives on Benefits and Costs," in A. G. Miller, ed., *The Social Psychology of Good and Evil*, 2nd ed. (New York: Guilford Press, 2016), 467–493; Peggy A. Thoits and Lyndi N. Hewitt, "Volunteer Work and Well-Being," *Journal of Health and Social Behavior* 42 (2001): 115–31.

3. Tim Kasser. *The High Price of Materialism* (Cambridge, MA: MIT Press, 2002); Tim Kasser, "Materialistic Values and Goals," *Annual Review of Psychology* 67 (2016): 489–514.

4. Ladd Wheeler and Kunitate Miyake, "Social Comparison in Everyday Life," *Journal of Personality and Social Psychology* 62, no. 5 (1992): 760.

5. Carl R. Rogers, "The Necessary and Sufficient Conditions of Therapeutic Personality Change," *Journal of Consulting Psychology* 21, no. 2 (1957): 95.

6. R. Nozick, *Anarchy, State, and Utopia* (New York: Basic Books, 1974).

7. Raymond S. Nickerson, "Confirmation Bias: A Ubiquitous Phenomenon in Many Guises," *Review of General Psychology* 2, no. 2 (1998): 175–220.

8. The psychological term for this is "egocentric bias." Kruger and Dunning, "Unskilled and Unaware of It," 1121.

9. "Philosophy bro" is the high-minded jargon of my field; it basically refers to a mansplaining, hotshot philosopher who doesn't listen to anyone else.

CHAPTER 5. VALUES IN AN UNFAIR CULTURE

1. Bourree Lam, "The Socialization of Women and the Gender Gap," *The Atlantic,* August 10, 2016, https://www .theatlantic.com/notes/2016/08/the-socialization-of -women/495200/; Shelley Coverman, "Gender, Domestic Labor Time, and Wage Inequality," *American Sociological Review* 48, no. 5 (1983): 623–37.

2. Sometimes attributed to Eleanor Roosevelt, but actually said by Pulitzer Prize–winning historian Laurel Thatcher Ulrich.

3. "'Man Up': How a Fear of Appearing Feminine Restricts Men, and Affects Us All," *Hidden Brain*, National Public Radio, 1 October 2018, https://www.npr.org/transcripts /653339162.

4. Jennifer K. Bosson et al., "Precarious Manhood and Displays of Physical Aggression," *Personality and Social Psychology Bulletin* 35, no. 5 (June 2009): 623–34, https://doi .org/10.1177/0146167208331161.

5. Jonathan Malesic argues that the strongly enculturated role of breadwinner for men is in conflict with both work and parenting goals. Malesic, *The End of Burnout: Why*

Work Drains Us and How to Build Better Lives (Oakland: University of California Press, 2022).

CHAPTER 6. WHEN ALL ELSE FAILS

1. Imposter syndrome, for those who haven't had the pleasure of its acquaintance, is the name for feelings of self-doubt and incompetence that persist despite objective achievements and qualifications. It is rampant in academia.
2. This is often called the problem of "adaptive preferences." Serene J. Khader, *Adaptive Preferences and Women's Empowerment* (Oxford: Oxford University Press, 2011); Nussbaum, *Women and Human Development*.
3. Tara Westover, *Educated* (New York: Random House, 2018).

CHAPTER 7. THE VALUE OF OTHERS

1. Joseph Henrich, *The Secret of Our Success: How Culture Is Driving Human Evolution, Domesticating Our Species, and Making Us Smarter* (Princeton: Princeton University Press, 2015).
2. You can see this in the many books on well-being already cited in these notes. For one additional example from a philosopher who defends an "objective list" of goods that enhance well-being, see Guy Fletcher, "A Fresh Start for the Objective-List Theory of Well-Being," *Utilitas* 25, no. 2 (2013): 206–20.
3. Paul Bloom gives a very clear explanation of what's wrong with this idea (often called "psychological hedonism") in his book *The Sweet Spot: The Pleasures of Suffering and the Search for Meaning* (New York: Ecco, 2021). Bloom offers

a compelling defense of what he calls "motivational pluralism." On nonegoistic motives in particular, see also Charles Daniel Batson, *Altruism in Humans* (New York: Oxford University Press, 2011) and Robert Kurzban, Maxwell N. Burton-Chellew, and Stuart A. West. "The Evolution of Altruism in Humans," *Annual Review of Psychology* 66 (2015): 575–99.

4. Caroline R. Lavelock et al., "The Quiet Virtue Speaks: An Intervention to Promote Humility," *Journal of Psychology and Theology* 42, no. 1 (2014): 99–110.

5. Epictetus, *The Enchiridion*, trans. Thomas W. Higginson (New York: Liberal Arts Press, 1948).

6. Joseph R. Biden, *Promise Me, Dad: A Year of Hope, Hardship, and Purpose* (New York: Flatiron Books, 2017), 33.

CHAPTER 8. FULFILLING OUR VALUES . . . MORALLY

1. David Hume, *A Treatise of Human Nature*, 2nd ed., Book 3: *Of Morals*, ed. L. A. Selby Bigge (Oxford: Oxford University Press, 1978), 589.

2. I also teach them the arguments against this form of relativism, which are very compelling. A good introduction can be found in Russ Shafer-Landau's *The Fundamentals of Ethics*, 5th ed. (Oxford: Oxford University Press, 2020).

3. Kiley J. Hamlin and Karen Wynn, "Young Infants Prefer Prosocial to Antisocial Others," *Cognitive Development* 26, no. 1 (2011): 30–39; Paul Bloom, *Just Babies: The Origins of Good and Evil* (New York: Broadway Books, 2013).

4. Thoits and Hewitt, "Volunteer Work and Well-Being"; Jane Allyn Piliavin, "Doing Well by Doing Good: Benefits for the Benefactor," in *Flourishing: The Positive Personality and the Life Well Lived*, ed. C. L. M. Keyes and J. Haidt

(Washington, DC: American Psychological Association, 2003), 227–47.

5. Elizabeth W. Dunn, Lara B. Aknin, and Michael I. Norton, "Spending Money on Others Promotes Happiness," *Science* 319, no. 5870 (2008): 1687–88.

6. Lyubomirsky, *How of Happiness*, 89–101, 125–37.

7. Netta Weinstein and Richard M. Ryan. "When Helping Helps: Autonomous Motivation for Prosocial Behavior and Its Influence on Well-Being for the Helper and Recipient," *Journal of Personality and Social Psychology* 98, no. 2 (2010): 222.

8. On US food insecurity: https://www.ers.usda.gov/topics/food-nutrition-assistance/food-security-in-the-us/key-statistics-graphics.aspx. On malaria in children: https://www.againstmalaria.com/. On climate change: https://www.oxfamamerica.org/explore/issues/climate-action/.

9. Some philosophers take the fact that Utilitarianism is so demanding to be a serious objection to it as a moral theory. See Samuel Scheffler, *The Rejection of Consequentialism: A Philosophical Investigation of the Considerations Underlying Rival Moral Conceptions*, revised ed. (Oxford: Clarendon Press, 1994); and Susan Wolf, "Moral Saints," *The Journal of Philosophy* 79, no. 8 (1982): 419–39.

10. Rule Utilitarianism is a type of utilitarianism that focuses on identifying the right set of rules, rather than the right action. It takes the right action to be the one that follows those optimific rules. Brad Hooker, *Ideal Code, Real World: A Rule-Consequentialist Theory of Morality* (Oxford: Oxford University Press, 2002).

11. Peter Singer, *The Life You Can Save* (New York: Pan Macmillan, 2010); Peter Singer, *The Most Good You Can Do* (New Haven, CT: Yale University Press, 2015).

12. John Rawls. *A Theory of Justice*, revised ed. (Cambridge, MA: Harvard University Press, 1999), 374.

13. Csikszentmihalyi. *Flow*, 61.

14. A charity website called Giving Multiplier (https://givingmultiplier.org/) capitalizes on this idea: it lets potential donors choose a cause that is personally meaningful and matches the contribution with a donation to an effective charity. The emphasis on "effective" comes from the effective altruism movement, which promotes donating money where it will have the greatest impact: https://www.effectivealtruism.org/. See also https://www.givewell.org/, an impact-focused charity evaluator.

15. Jean-Paul Sartre, *Existentialism Is a Humanism* (New Haven, CT: Yale University Press, 2007).

CONCLUSION

1. My wording here is inspired by Christine Korsgaard. In her *Sources of Normativity* (Cambridge: Cambridge University Press, 1996), she argues that our reflective minds are the solution to the problem of the authority of reason.

INDEX

DISCUSSION QUESTIONS

1. In chapter 1, Valerie Tiberius writes, "The way that we pursue a good life—no matter how it is defined—is by having goals, figuring out plans for attaining them, and acting on those plans." What goals do you have that are most relevant to improving your life or increasing your well-being?

2. Valerie Tiberius offers five strategies for understanding and improving your values and goals: introspection, the lab rat strategy, guided reflection, learning from others, and exploration. Which strategies have you tried? What do you find works best for you and why?

3. Have you ever given up on a goal? Why?

4. Valerie Tiberius tells us how she learned to value "play," even though she didn't before. Is there anything you should value that you don't currently? Or something you should value more than you do?

5. Think about ways that your community or culture has shaped your values. Is there an example when this conflicted with what you really think is most important in life?

6. Are some values better than others?

7. Have someone else's values ever conflicted with your own? How have you resolved these conflicts?

8. Valerie Tiberius focuses primarily on two main questions in *What Do You Want Out of Life?*: How do we identify our values and goals and recognize conflicts between them? And also, how can our values and goals be improved so we can manage these conflicts and promote greater fulfillment? During your reading of the text, did you focus on these questions? What did you conclude?